Published by

Emma Technologies, LLC
Quincy, MA 02169
emmatech.us


Library of Congress Catalog Number: 2014903335
Copyright 2009, 2018 © by Jeremy Cope


All Rights Reserved
Printed in the United States of America
Third Edition, April 2018


4  17  10  27  13  40

To the mothers in our life, real and maternal.
And to **Her**,
my existing proof that *angels live amongst us*.
May we all acknowledge that we wouldn't be
where we are today without some assistance.

# LESSON PLAN

# Mission Statement

*At Project 27, we strive to represent the goals and interests of the American **CO**mmon **PE**ople. We recognize that in order to achieve progress, we must make agreements, sometimes compromising desires and ideals. But our core values are what bind us together, and allow us to make sacrifices along the way, knowing we will always be there for each other.*

# Welcome, Let's Begin

*And so, my fellow Americans: ask not what your country can do for you — ask what you can do for your country.*

-President John F. Kennedy

Throughout our history as a young nation, America has overcome challenges and adversity in order to protect our greatest values: equality and individual rights. We have made it our responsibility to protect these ideals throughout the globe, through use of our economic, cultural, and military influence. At these times of uncertainty in the world it is essential that we re-affirm our faith in America and all that she stands strongly for.

Unfortunately our government is failing us. It's been auctioned off through capitalism and turned into a powerful, but inefficient organization.

Luckily for us we still stand a chance. Our Founding Fathers gave its citizens the ultimate power and God bless them for that. The simple, yet extraordinary right to vote has an infinite ability to change the system. But change isn't going to come through some Senator from Illinois; true change will come from the ingenuity of the American individual. After all, it was an American who wrote the Constitution; an American who led us out of the Civil War; and an American who stood before thousands with a Dream.

But change can only be accomplished if we stick together. We are a country made up of mothers and fathers, brothers and sisters, friends and neighbors. It is time we settle our differences and embrace each other as a nation. We are only as strong as the weakest link when hatred tears us apart.

Thus, we owe it to ourselves to have an honest and open discussion. Was there not a debate before the Constitution was written? At some point though, compromises were made by both sides for the sake of progress and getting things done.

What we present to you here is a set of lessons, 27 of them in all, for us to read through and discuss together. In order for us to bond and get along, we cannot be afraid to discuss the tough topics. What role should America play in the world? What is an Abortion? Are we proud of our Education System? If we cannot talk about these issues, and come to an agreement, then we as a nation risk losing it all.

Before we begin, let us introduce you to a few themes that will be resonating throughout these lessons. These themes are based on the ideals of our Founding Fathers, and on our faith in the individual rights we are born with.

**The Right To Choose.** We have guaranteed ourselves the freedom of choice that comes with being an American. We have opinions and make decisions without prosecution from the government or harmful force. Some choices we take for granted, like what to eat or wear. Others we take pride in, like where to live or what career to pursue. But there are also choices we hope to never make: the choice to terminate a pregnancy, or to take one's life. It is part of America's foundation that we are given this freedom and it is our duty and responsibility to embrace this liberty.

**Our United States.** We all share common borders, yet they all represent a different background of culture and ideas. Every State is unique and enacts laws that compliment the soul of the region. These differences allow the people of the State to vote in confidence, knowing their distinct principles will be represented in the government. The power of authority must be given back to the states with the federal government only enforcing guidelines; *let the people run their city.*

**Erica.** A young fictional character, she will be following us along this journey and help us gain prospective. Throughout a few lessons, we will watch as policy takes place and the tough decisions we confront throughout our lives. We really think you are going to end up enjoying her.

Each lesson will outline a topic for us to ponder and discuss. We will search for the truth, and establish requirements for a solution. As American Citizens, we are all in this together and must find the common ground among us.

Now more than ever, we must double down on the American ideals, and re-invest in the American Dream. After all, it was the American Dream that produced a Thomas Edison, a Martin Luther King Jr., and a Steve Jobs. While we might not all become icons, we can take pride in knowing it was our culture, our nation, our blood that produced the individual who had The Dream. We would be foolish to ignore our potential.

But we also must hold our government more accountable. The current dysfunction with our officials has lead to an extreme lack of trust. There is a certain expectation of quality and service when so much has been sacrificed for the sake of our society. Either our government will attempt to fix the mess they created, or we as citizens must speak up and utilize our voting power. The government works for us, the citizens; we must not let that be forgotten.

So at this time in America's crossroads, it has never been more important for us to stand together and define who we are. Too often we are distracted by the achievements of today, that we get lost and forget the big picture. We might be a young nation, but our faith and our principles of equality will triumphant and stand the test of time; **this we are sure of.**

Now, let us all take a few minutes to take a step back and reflect with some personal time. Go relax, grab your favorite drink, perhaps a snack, and join us on this journey as we explore America and what she will become.

## NOTES

---

*We have left some space at the end of each section for you, the reader to take notes and jot down your thoughts. Remember, we are only starting the conversation; it is up to you, the American Citizen, to ponder and discuss. Enjoy!*

# E.D.U

*I have never let my schooling interfere with my education.*

-Mark Twain

Education. Most Americans take it for granted. We are told that if we work hard and attend class, doors of opportunity will open. And yes, there are the success stories, but we must not overlook the ones our education system has failed the most: the street gangs, runaways, and addicts. Our nation's education needs to he taken more seriously and not as competitively.

But, it all starts with the teachers. The recognition given to them is certainly not enough. Collectively, they spend the most time with our children and help mold us together as a nation. We should take pride in our education system and the people that run it. We should be ashamed it fell to the world's 8th best education system. **This is America**.

Education reform will require evaluating all aspects of the system. From the moment a child steps on the bus in the morning, to the time the student takes off their pads after a football game; these are all teaching moments in their life. To take education reform seriously, we need to value it for what it is in our society.

Today, most parents are employed full-time, or would be if the jobs were available. When the closing school bell rings at 2 pm, we cut our labor pool short and forgo valuable teaching opportunities. The school system should embrace the new American workforce and provide adequate programs for our students all day long.

As former students, we appreciate not wanting to extend class time, and nor should we. But after-school programs do not have to stay in the classroom to be effective. We've seen positive results with after-school clubs, sporting events, and even naptime for the young ones. All of these activities should be encouraged, but never required; to deprive kids of after-school neighborhood hide and seek would be unacceptable.

And we must continue to place emphasis and value on vacation and family time. It is not until you join the workforce do you realize the grim reality of never having a three-month break again. Vacations offer families the time to spend together and if fortunate enough, the ability to travel around this beautiful country of ours. Traveling our country provides unique learning experiences and bonds us closer as a nation with our memories.

But, it all starts with the teachers. We need to be able to provide better recognition for those teachers that preform well, and hold those that don't to a higher standard. If we are having trouble securing quality teachers, then we should create a guaranteed minimum salary. Every one of us can recall a teacher in our life that inspired us to greatness, but we would be hard-pressed to identify one in our local community today. We need to give these individuals more recognition and respect if we are going to expect so much of them in taking care of our own. Community appreciation can go a long way in thanking someone.

But with all teaching moments in life there exists

accountability and we cannot continue to allow poor performing teachers to manage classes. Let us create teacher report cards, ones that are available freely to the public; allow us as a community to evaluate and respect our teachers. We should be aware of their strengths, interests, and the ways they are working to improve.

But it is not just the teachers that need to be reviewed and held more accountable, but also the system itself. We need a curriculum that teaches our students the skills of the 21st century, otherwise, we as a nation, will continue to fall behind. While we reform our education system, we must also look to make investments in modernizing the tools and teaching techniques.

For some students, one-on-one tutoring is the best way to learn, others thrive in a group setting. Every student is different and therefore should be selected individually for that class type and teaching style. This will require an adaptive system, one where we no longer group our students by age, but rather by learning abilities and maturity. We need to be able to cater the education system to the individual but without loosing the dynamics of group learning.

The demand for a better education system should not be disputed. How to achieve this will certainly raise a debate. But we must be decisive and act swiftly, for every year we graduate with a failing system, is another difficult one down the road for our workforce. If we utilize the summer break better to perform re-evaluations and adjustments, we can make rapid improvements over the short term and into the future. And if reform is successful enough, we may be fortunate one day to provide services and education year round to the entire American population.

## NOTES

*What do you think?*

# ECO 101

*In our personal ambitions we are individualists. But in our seeking for economic and political progress as a nation, we all go up or else we all go down as one people.*

-President Franklin D. Roosevelt

Emerging from World War II with America and it's ideals the victor, our economy flourished, taking advantage of American ingenuity and the hard work and dedication of our society. Undoubtedly we have run into some rough patches, being squeezed in the late seventies by the oil shortages, and more recently the housing crash that led to the Great Recession. But for the most part the United States has been able to use its economic power to help influence and protect our principles of equality. This has also enabled us to enjoy the other side of the economic coin: the stability and security of a financial market to plan retirement on.

Over the past 15 years however, something has changed and we need to accept that we are no longer the powerhouse in the world we once where. Countries like China, Brazil, and India spent that past half century studying and learning from us. A deeper recession and continued austerity in Europe can lead to a stagnant market and wipe our retirement funds clean. The idea that we live in a world economy is not new, but our weaning power and influence over it is something we must learn to cope with.

As with every challenge presented to this wonderful country, there is a silver lining that will allow us to overcome and once again rise to the top. However, we must start with managing our expectations and understanding the problem at hand. We no longer have the biggest ship in the economic ocean, and can no longer control the market waters of the seas. But

America will always have the most sought after vessel through which we can navigate and create waves in our wake. For it has never been our shear strength that has guaranteed success, but our wits and ingenuity to overcome the obstacles placed in front of us.

So let us assess the damage and current state of our economic ship after years of neglect. Ever since 1976 when our currency was taken off the gold standard, we have been forced to rely on our emotions to lead the way for stability. As the Iraq War has taught us dearly, it is not wise to make decisions when emotions run high and facts can be misinterpreted. We can no longer rely on the government to maintain and provide a healthy, stable economy.

Many would argue that our nation's recovery from the Great Recession of 2007 was due to assistance from our government. But to those that put in the extra effort or worked longer hours without pay, the American recovery was lifted on the shoulders of the working individual. It was the sacrifices and hard work by the American workers that recovered our nation. That is our silver lining, the proof we need to move forward: a collected effort by a group, the American workers, will always be able to achieve more than a group of individuals acting alone. And Washington has been just the opposite: a group of characters with no common purpose or accord to help us move forward.

That is not to say we are flawless; our ability as Americans to consume with a never-ending appetite has made us want more and with less patience. We no longer have the ability to wait for the evening news; it must be delivered to us instantly or fear being left behind. We expect food to taste better, cost less, and take less time to prepare. In order to capitalize on our nation's economic momentum, we must all start managing our expectations and stop indulging in our selfish desires. As a country, we are only as rich as our poorest minority, and as strong as our weakest child. If the last few years have taught us anything, it is that we are in this together, one nation that stands strong and prevails at the threat of danger.

But, while our nation recovered, the privileged seemed untouched while everyone else was stuck at the bottom. If we are going to continue to pull together and navigate the economic waters, we must address this financial discrepancy in a serious manner. The monopoly on wealth we have allowed capitalism to create will put our entire country at risk of sinking. We must demand policies from our government that provide incentives for those at the top to reinvest in the skilled hard workers at the bottom. As the land of opportunity, we must guarantee that every American has a fair chance at climbing the economic ladder.

Additionally, as we go through these social and economic changes, we must also focus on the monopolies and market regimes that have formed a strong influence over our nation. Capitalism has led to prosperity for many organizations, but it has also provided them with unnecessary influence over decisions made by the American individual. The

American workers are the powerhouse of our economy; direction and policy dictated by the power of our vote. However challenging it may seem to battle the establishments of our economy, the American voter and society must act in order to protect our future prosperity.

To influence these market regimes we must present to them America's silver lining and provide incentives for them to double down on American ingenuity. Ever since Apollo and Armstrong first landed down on the moon, there should be no doubt there is only one place in this world where no problem is too big to be solved: **America**. We should encourage companies to unload offshore accounts and spend it on American creativity. Subsidies should be set up with the sole purpose of developing and productizing the next great opportunity. The American workforce and our collective effort are too big to fail.

We have shown as a country, time and time again, that we are able to outperform our competitive allies because of our ingenuity and freedom to express new and original ideas. With the strength of the American workforce behind us, we will be able to accomplish anything we put our minds to.

## NOTES

*A penny for your thoughts:*

# In Congress We Trust

*We the people are the rightful masters of both Congress and the courts, not to overthrow the Constitution, but to overthrow the men who pervert the Constitution.*

-President Abraham Lincoln

*Senator, with all due respect, what drugs are you on and why aren't you sharing them with the rest of this country? You misinterpret the truth and behave as if you are hallucinating. We, as the citizens that have voted you into power **deserve better and demand more.***

In reality, no single individual has broken our government, but collectively each member has allowed the downfall to continue.

Members of Congress are like managers the employees get to vet and elect for the position. Yet unlike a boss, if things go horribly wrong, we can replace them. Still for some reason, every six years, we fail to live up to our potential as voters. The problem lies therefor not just with the people we have elected to serve us, but with the rules of the system we have allowed them to create.

In 1787 when the Constitution was written, a blueprint was provided on how our government should be structured with checks and balances. No one could have predicted just how corrupt things could get. Our Founding Fathers gave us the ultimate power to check and balance our government free of abuse. Far too long we have failed to use that power and if we wait much longer, we may lose that ability all together.

Ultimately, the power to fix the system lies with the people. It is this quest of freedom from tyranny and persecution that has led to many of our internal struggles as a country: from national independence with the American Revolution, to ending slavery with our Civil War. These internal battles have defined us as a nation, yet all stemmed with the American people demanding equality. History has taught us that if we choose to stick together, we can overcome this injustice and once again restore faith in the system.

We must not forget however, the importance of a representative government and the benefits to having elected officials we can trust. Even with the advent of the digital age, and the increased speed of information, there still exists benefits in having a few focus intently on taking care of the rest. The problem lies not with a representative system, but with our current implementation. We can no longer allow a limitless government to implement our Founding Father's blueprint. A few small changes will go a long way in restoring the checks and balances our Constitution was set up to ensure:

We must first start with term limits to members of Congress. This policy has been effective with the President of the United States and should be applied to the legislative branch as well.

We must reserve the right to recall representatives on a national level. Elected by a region, members of Congress have been endowed to make decisions on behalf of the rest of us. It would be foolish to not be able to impeach an official when a misuse of power occurs.

We must also address the privileges our

Congress has entitled to itself. A cut of government programs without touching the salary of Congress represents a problem with our country. An official, who sits in an office and receives better benefits than our soldiers on the front lines, represents what is wrong with our country.

We must also institute a zero tolerance policy towards corruption and abuse of power. Not until we elect honest officials, can we establish trust with our government system.


Ultimately, we must remind Congress that they are employees of the system and work for the citizens of the United States. We have a Congress set up with One House Of Representatives and One Senate, not 256 Representatives and 100 Senators. If the current members refuse to work together to tackle our country's pressing issues, then society must work hard to find a team of people who can.

We as voters deserve to know more about our official's agendas and daily activities. No one is forced into Congress and officials must be held to a higher standard if they want to continue to represent us. We should require an open lifestyle of our representatives that will free us from the scandals that distract our nation. There must be a renewed openness to representing us; one that clarifies how decisions are being made that affect our lives.

We can also create mechanisms to make Congress more effective. Rather than work together to tackle our problems, our leaders have been focused on limiting the ability of the other political party. This approach is short sighted and has prevented a functional government. In effect, rules of the general assembly of Congress should be nullified if it is determined to hinder or interfere with the principles of democracy. To talk indefinitely in order to prevent action represents what is wrong with our country. A yay or nay vote is better than no vote at all.

So unless we stand up to Congress, and remind them that they have sworn to protect the Constitution, we will continue to be abused and taken advantage of by the system. But we must be able to trust Congress to make decisions on behalf of the rest of us, or risk democracy failing us. For it is the power of the vote that enables us to correct the injustice and disarray that has festered in our government for way to long.

# NOTES

*Try representing your thoughts as words:*

# The Legend of John Smith

*Because of what America is and what America has done, a firmer courage, a higher hope, inspires the heart of all humanity.*

*-President Calvin Coolidge*

The Greatest American you could have ever met was fittingly named John Smith. He was a World War II veteran, a High School English teacher, and a loving parent. His accomplishments in life never landed him on the cover a Wheaties box, but in a sense, that makes him all the more special. And for that reason alone, we owe it to ourselves to strive to be better citizens and continue our nations legacy of becoming something great.

To say he was an inspiration and a model we can all strive to become would be an understatement. John Smith not only lived as a member of one of the greatest generations our country has ever produced, but he also exemplified it like many of that time did. Born into the Great Depression, our country was going through tough times. High unemployment, rapid inflation, and long food lines created daily struggles. But rather than point blame, and expect their problems to be solved, John Smith and his generation worked as one to rebuild our foundation and assemble a strong unity.

Struggling through the Great Depression should be all we have to ask of one generation, but for John Smith and his fellow Americans, our country required an additional sacrifice. The demands of World War II were requested out of necessity, rather than desire. It was a war unlike wars fought today, not driven by political or economic reasons, but one required to prevent the extermination of our entire race. John Smith, like so many other Americans, was willing and courageous to stand up to the evil that festered during those years. *We are forever indebted.*

After the war and coming home, there were many career paths our soldiers chose to pursue. Many utilized life skills taught during service. Others attended college and furthered their education. After reconnecting with his future wife, John Smith went on to study American literature at Hobart College. As if rebuilding after the Great Depression or joining the Navy to fight in WWII was not enough, John Smith wanted to leave a lasting influence and choose to become a High School English teacher.

To become a teacher is more than just getting a job, and showing up 9 to 5; a teacher exemplifies and sets the standard for what it means to give back to society without asking much in return. For decades, John Smith, like so many others, stood in front of students and inspired greatness. Many passed through his class, becoming lawyers or scientists, and continuing to lay the foundation for our post-World War II generation. If we claim our children, and therefore the students of our classrooms, are the future of this country, then the teachers are laying the brickwork.

When it came time to start a family and raise kids of his own, John Smith and his wife, Emma, had difficulty in getting pregnant. Rather then become discouraged and give up, the two of them decided to adopt children, and like many times before, give the best effort they could. Adopting and raising children embodies the fabric of our society and helps bond us together as citizens. John Smith and his wife Emma once again gave back to society without asking for much in return. His love and life lessons taught, not just to his students, but now his children as well, have left an ever-lasting impression on all.

If you walk down to the National Mall in Washington, DC, you will not find a monument for John Smith, and nor should there ever be. We as citizens do not require a statue to honor great Americans; rather we should memorialize them in our behavior. Opening the door for the strangers, saying thank you, wishing a good day to someone; there are many small things we can all do on a daily basis that not only brighten someone else's day, but also requires little effort. If John Smith was able to spend his entire life fighting wars and rebuilding our country, then we as Americans can perform the simple task of being friendlier to each other.

Giving unconditionally to this country was something that came naturally to John Smith. Like many others born in his generation, the sacrifices made and commitment to our values has enabled America to be prosperous for the decades that followed their careers. If we are compelled to leave a country for our children, then we must honor and continue to fulfill the hard work dedicated to us. Their contributions to society should not go unrecognized, and nor shall they be only remembered in the history books. To truly embrace and memorialize The Greatest American, we as a society must give back to each other and put a stop to the blame game that has engulfed our lives. Too often we are quick to judge and point figures at each other that we forget we are brothers and sisters and stand as one.

If John Smith could leave only one legacy, it would be his commitment to future generations. By passing on knowledge and leading by good example, John Smith was able to ensure we would be able to enjoy life to an extent that perhaps he never would. It is his unselfishness we should honor and continue in order to sustain this beautiful country of ours, The United States of America.

## NOTES

*An American walked into a bar...*

# Emergency Room

*America's health care system is neither healthy,
caring, nor a system.*

*-Walter Cronkite*

$R$ick, a proud father of three, was recently diagnosed with cancer. He had lived a healthy lifestyle his entire life, never smoking, exercising multiple times a week, and eating with a nutrition plan in mind--that is why the prognosis was so hard to understand. *He was given 3 months to live.*

Susan grew up in a divorced household and as a by-product turned into an alcoholic. She was in and out of the hospitals, ranging from broken bones to recently diagnosed liver disease. She had no means to pay for the hospital bills, but she was still taken care of when in need. *She now lives a clean life in a shelter on 5th St.*

In the end, not even the best health care system can change fate. However, we must ensure basic care to our American citizens in need. As we learned in the Great Recession of 2007, we rise and fall in the country as one. If we commit to take care of ourselves, we can all benefit from a healthier system and gain more than we put in. Using the economics of our population, as well as the vast databases of information, we should be able to provide better services at a lower cost to all whom participate. Unfortunately the quality and efficiency of the current system is in dire repair.

The health industry represents 12% of our nations economy and impacts us all on a personal level. For the well being of the American citizen, we must demand and provide a more conscience and efficient health care system. Health care laws are social contracts to ensure we take care of each other, without dictating each other's health care decisions, like treatments and diets. But by creating guidelines, we can create a better quality of life as well as ensure that everybody does their part to contribute.

Ultimately however, it is the individual's obligation to maintain a healthy, sustained lifestyle. While we may desire to impose decisions on society, we must respect a citizen's freedom of choice. We are a nation where we may do as we please, as long as we do not harm each other. It is that definition of harm, that seems to divide us at times.

Undoubtedly, the health care system is a morally charged issue. Every aspect of a law seems to dictate a lifestyle. Our Founding Fathers never envisioned a system that could impose on our daily lives. But our Founding Fathers would have also never envisioned our nation's great prosperity and the responsibility that comes with it. We have stuck together, battled the challenges abroad, everyone sacrificing so that the common good of America can improve generation by generation. If we commit to take care of each other, we can continue this tradition of prosperity, and strengthen ourselves for the challenges ahead.

Daily an American is diagnosed with a disease of which the treatment is unaffordable. We are a nation that has cured diseases that where once a death wish; yet we cannot provide these cures to those in need. **We must do better.**

But this also touches upon a general theme

within the health care system. If someone comes into the Emergency Room, but cannot afford treatment, should we provide them care? There may be many improvements to the system we can make, but only a couple of requirements to ensure the answer is yes.

**It must be Affordable.** The only thing worse than a broken system, is a broken expensive system. Those who cannot afford care will be supported by the rest, so we must ensure it does not create too much of a burden.

**It must be Available.** There should be many programs to choose from and no one should ever be turned away. Living a healthy lifestyle should not require sitting in waiting rooms and filling out forms. We have become more efficient at fixing our cars and computers than we have with ourselves.

Fortunately, the tools are all here to build an impressive health care system for our nation. Advances in robotics have allowed some of the most difficult surgeries to be preformed. The personal touch of nurses may one-day transition us back to house calls, rather then bottle all sick people up in one building. Whatever advances lie ahead, we must always strive to improve the quality of life for all Americans.

But, ultimately there will be those who refuse to follow any recommendation concerning their health. There will be those who develop diseases due to the fact that they made a choice discouraged by society. We cannot ignore these individuals, yet we cannot impose a lifestyle on them. However, through social pressure we can discourage unhealthy behavior and use the power of the consumer to ensure a healthy alternative.

Above all it comes down to the freedom of choice to decide how your body should be treated and taken care for. We all have different insights and opinions on personal care. Unfortunately, we will all die one day; how we get there, and the ending we play, should be our own choice.

## *NOTES*

*Care to share your thoughts?*

# American Tolls

*In 1790, the nation which had fought a revolution against taxation without representation discovered that some of its citizens weren't much happier about taxation **with** representation.*

-President Lyndon B. Johnson

In 1773 a revolution was ignited by a discussion of taxes. The British were taxing common household items, such as tea and paper, and the Colonizers where not pleased with the representation they received. They expected freedom of speech, the right to self-rule, and protection. Thus the American Revolution erupted out of lack of trust for the governing establishment.

Centuries later, we as Americans are still paying taxes into a flawed system and receiving incompetence in return. While another bloody revolution is not upon us, it is up to us to fix a broken system and restore faith in it.

As with most complicated issues, there are two main components to this story. One involves the collection methods, the other deals with spending; leaving the budget to blur the line. For now, we will focus on our government's revenue, paying attention to taxes and our citizen's contributions.

Let us first define income as value added to your wealth, regardless of source. For our discussion, if you started the year with $10 in your bank account, and the following year began with $20, then your income for the year was $10. You also managed to survive a year in America with only $10. The point is income is income is income.

Investments and capital gain add to your wealth and should be treated just the same. To treat income differently, based on its source, is anything but fair.

Americans all have different skills and talents to contribute in a beneficial way for society. It is discriminatory to vary tax rates based on the type of investments being made. We can reference a Farmer purchasing a tracker for his farm, or a Wall Street banker creating derivative funds.

Ultimately, the burden of the tax revenue should be fairly distributed among all American citizens. However, there are other ways we as individuals can contribute back into society with having to discuss money or income:

Those that have served in our military forces deserve the utmost respect and gratitude from the rest of American society. Many have sacrificed themselves physically, while many more have been left to cope with the mental anxiety caused by conflict. Therefor their tax responsibility should be less during and after duty.

Government employees on the other hand have not nearly given back as much, yet they run the system and work for the people. After all, does it make sense to tax Congress, only to turn around and pay the President? Therefor their tax responsibility should be less during employment.

Finally that leaves us, the American individuals earning our living through capitalism. We are the fabric of society, and it is up to the rest of us to hold it together. How to evenly divide the burden however has not always been any easy discussion.

What seems fair then is to evenly distribute the tax responsibility among different groups of individuals. We can streamline our current tax brackets by assembling into larger groups and creating a cleaner flat tax based on our financial obligations. For example, we could require the top 1% to evenly cover 10% of our nation's tax burden.

By simplifying the system, we will be able to remove these so called loopholes and give every American citizen the opportunity to improve their financial status. Only when we all are contributing fairly, can we move up on the economic ladder.

We must also recognize that corporations are not people and should not be treated as such. While at times they require healthcare, in the form of subsidies and bailouts, they are not citizens with a pulse. They have the ability to amass greater wealth and power than any individual can on their own. To that extent, American corporations should be expected to contribute more than the American workers they employ. The corporate financial burden should be even distributed amongst the industries with a fair and predictable rate.

Additionally, we should require foreign individuals and corporations operating inside our country to be taxed higher. Entities that have not pledged an oath to America should be taxed appropriately to compensate for our sacrifices that has enabled their success.

Taxes and contributions to society help fund and support the re-investment in America. But only if we are willing to tear down the current system, and simplify the contributions, then we can all thrive and prosper as one. Perhaps then, tax statements amongst politicians wouldn't be so private; as they would all have a similar one to share.

## NOTES

*Thoughts and opinions will always be free:*

# Drug Wars

*'We are losing the war against drugs.' You know what that implies? There's a war being fought and the people on drugs are winning it.*

-Bill Hicks

The current status of drug abuse within our country is appalling. We all see it on a daily basis, whether on the corner of a city block, or in the front page of entertainment news. Yet we turn a blind eye and pretend that these issues do not affect us, that substance abuse only affects users; we say ignorance can be just as dangerous.

In our current system of Drug Policy, we have more people incarcerated for drug related charges than we do for violent crimes. We spend more on drug suppression than we do on violence and terrorism prevention. Further, we have allowed the pharmaceutical companies to introduce and manufacture stronger, easier to conceal substances. It is absurd that we have allowed prescribed drugs to infiltrate the black market and lead to a devastating epidemic. The blame however lies with more than just the users and abusers.

We as society failed in creating clear policies that local and state government can adhere to and enforce. A legalized substance on the state level that is considered a felony to possess on the national level only leads to confusion and overhead. We must coordinate the policies and re-evaluate the criminal punishments for drug possession. Surely those that enable abuse of substances should be held more accountable than those that have been sucked into addiction. But at the end of the day, who benefits when a teenager becomes addicted to legally manufactured painkillers?

But there are also economic factors that influence our Drug Policy. Opportunities and industries are created in researching drugs; products taxed and regulated. A re-evaluation of our nations' Drug Policy could lead to more revenue and jobs in the manufacturing, distribution, and consumption of legalized substances.

Already accepted by popular culture, marijuana has become the face of reforming our Drug Policy. Legal for medicinal purposes in a handful of states, a couple have even legalized its use for recreational purposes. Yet consumption and possession of marijuana is still considered illegal on the federal level, causing more conflicts in regulating substance abuse within our country. We will now evaluate an implementation of legalizing the consumption of marijuana:

To facilitate this discussion we will create four policies a State can implement: 1) Legal to grow or manufacture marijuana, 2) Legal to purchase or consume marijuana, 3) Legal to distribute or transport marijuana, and 4) A rejection of all the above and classify marijuana as an illegal substance.

**Policy 1.** Allow those States that have a history of farming and cultivating to participate in a legalization program, while not necessary enabling its residents. States like Ohio, Iowa, or the Dakotas may choose to participate in this category.

**Policy 2.** Appeals to States that have embraced marijuana use and wish to collect taxes and revenue on a substance that is already consumed within their borders. California, Colorado, and Washington would most likely adhere to this policy.

**Policy 3.** Those that wish to neither participate in the production or consumption of marijuana, but geographically lie in-between States that choose to. This will enable these States to collect taxes and help maintain their transportation infrastructure. States like Oregon, Wyoming, and Pennsylvania may benefit from this policy.

**Policy 4.** Marijuana is considered an illegal substance. All States will adhere to this by default; only through a voter-initiated bill should a State implement a different policy. This allows the federal government to set up guidelines and the State's residents to decide how to participate.

By creating opt-in reform, we will effectively roll out the legalization in stages and allow for competition as States set their own tax rates and policies. Each State's implementation will be reviewed and approved by the federal government; allowing each system to be balanced and monitored against our nation's best interests.

What makes America stand above the rest, are the individual freedoms we allow each State and its residents to employ. This way, Americans are free to choose where to reside and the rules of the state they live by. If reform is successful we could implement a similar system for other substances such as alcohol and tobacco. States like Utah may be in favor of banning the consumption of alcohol, while Indiana may want to collect more on the tobacco that is transported throughout its State.

At the end of the day however, we must be cautious. We cannot allow changes to our Drug Policy to be viewed as an endorsement of drug use. We must ensure that decriminalization of substances does not proliferate and become a pattern within American culture. But whatever the outcome, we cannot accept the status quo. Illicit and illegal drug use within our country has the ability to bring us down and tear apart the fabric of society we have worked so hard to protect.

# NOTES

*Your thoughts, on drugs:*

# America, Incarcerated

*To have once been a criminal is no disgrace. To remain a criminal is the disgrace.*

-Malcolm X

We are taught at a young age that crime does not pay; indeed, no one gains when a crime is committed. Those who are violent or take advantage of others are imprisoned and stripped of their rights. Criminals are removed from society and their choices severely limited.

But at what cost do we incarcerate these individuals? Convicted criminals are provided a shelter, as well as meals and personal care. The cost to society ends up being much greater than the original crime. Not only are we victims to the crime, but our system requires us to provide for criminals so that they are no longer physically integrated into our daily lives. We as society continue to pay for their crimes long after they are convicted.

Currently, there are few options with how to deal with the incarcerated. Proposed solutions include the death penalty and rehabilitation. The death penalty requires a well natured person to end ones life and we combat violence with more violence. Our current rehabilitation system however, is flawed; some people cannot be redeemed, while others will fall back onto bad habits. Only a small few are able to integrate back into society and lead successful, contributing lives. However, we can all agree that society would benefit more if fewer criminals were locked away feeding off the system. Therefore, we need to improve our rehabilitation efforts, and be able to integrate criminals safely back into society.

To re-evaluate our system, we must simplify the types of crimes and classify different tiers of criminals. Crimes against society break established rules; whether as minor as running a red light, or as horrific as murder. Currently crimes can be classified as felonies or misdemeanors. We propose the rest is far too complex and not always fair. America was born on the land of opportunity, a land of second chances and a fresh start. Most people deserve a second chance, and society should demand we are no longer responsible for those that have wronged us.

By simplifying the categories of crimes, we can better identify criminal risk. Depending on the nature of the initial crime individuals would be classified differently. For example, petty theft or a traffic violation would assume a low risk, while horrendous crimes, such as rape or human trafficking, would be higher risk. Individuals would move into higher risk categories as their crimes become more violent, while a progression towards rehabilitation would transition them back towards lower risk. This creates a system, and requires society, to be more accountable for preventing progression towards violence; as those in the highest risk category are harder to rehabilitate and in the long run cost society the most. Not all actions are redeem-able though; once determined a high enough risk, you cannot earn your way back.

When an individual commits a crime, they are taking something away from society, whether it is trivial such as an opportunity, or something horrific such as a life. Crimes create debt that must be paid back to the population. We as society should focus on the opportunity of the crime and demand more effort from the criminal in repayment to the innocent.

A well-established rehabilitation program can facilitate debt payments back to society. We can require individuals to work their way back into society by paying back the criminal debt. As one progresses through rehabilitation, the tasks can become more challenging, yet the reward more fulfilling. This will enable the individual and society to benefit from the completion of each step.

The idea of labor camps is often associated with repressive nations and generally frowned upon by human rights activists. However, elected physical labor must be better utilized. We must provide means for a criminal to give back to society using their mind and body as tools.

Rehabilitation programs can include physical labor such as producing energy or manufacturing cheap goods. We should also encourage furthering their education so that they can contribute to society in an intellectual way.

In the end, we must recognize that crimes cost

and affect not only the victims, but society as a whole. We can no longer remove and lock away this injustice. Rather we must attempt to benefit from those that have harmed us; as a criminal rehabilitates, society should also benefit. It can be in the form of tangible goods and services, or intellectually through education.

Ultimately, the current criminal system is creating too much of a burden on society and the benefits we have provided to the criminals can no longer continue. Call it a jail or public housing with a lock on the door, criminals and those who harm society, should be required to work off their debt. If we continue to facilitate this current state of protection and nourishment away from society, then there will be no incentive for them to rehabilitate and integrate back into the population. And we as society will continue to pay endlessly for their crimes.

# NOTES

*They can never take our words:*

# Ultimate Choice

*Give me liberty, or give me death!*

-Patrick Henry

*Erica had a drunk for a mother who beat her regularly. Her father was gone; left the family when she was young. She was bullied at school and had trouble fitting in with others. With her back against the wall and nowhere to go Erica laid out her options. At age 14, she made the ultimate choice and decided to end her life. That evening she walked into the Assisted Life Clinic and took matters into her own hands. If it weren't for a chat with the assistant prior to the procedure, she would have gone through with it. For it wasn't the mandatory pre-screening that persuaded her, but the kindness and caring she received from the attendant. Not everyone changes their mind here, but today, Erica was one of them.*

To end one's own life, or to commit suicide, is a decision that should never be taken lightly. No one benefits when a suicide occurs and the consequences are ultimate. Such behavior is discouraged by society through use of pop culture and support counseling. **Yet it still happens.**

However, there may be health reasons for choosing to end one's own life. Diseases such as A.L.S. and Parkinson's lead to a slow deteriorating death. Too often we require patients to suffer rather than enable them to choose. We should provide those who suffer an option for ending their pain. **Yet it never happens.**

Currently suicide and assisted suicide are

outlawed at a national level. Recently, a few States have assisted suicide for medical cases, but it's use is restricted. What value are we promoting when we outlaw a personal choice? We were all guaranteed a final day when put on this earth. Have we eliminated our freedom to decide when that day is?

Fortunately, there are many options to enable this freedom of choice without promoting the idea of taking action. Life is too valuable and we should do everything possible to save those around us. But rather than discourage and shun away from the topic, we should provide support and options at local clinics. With this, we may be able to save more lives and establish a better sense of trust.

At the federal level, guidelines should be put in place to determine what options and services can be provided at clinics. Each individual State will then have the choice to implement a system that meets the requirements or continue to outlaw assistance all together. The federal government will only coordinate policies and set minimum requirements for the States that choose to participate.

For example, it should be required that an individual must meet with a certified doctor prior to a procedure. This will help establish intent and provide suggestions for other medical treatments. Also, a grace period should be set up in order to prevent spontaneous decisions. We would not be fulfilling our duty as a society if we did not try to save each life. This is about giving choices back to the individuals, but in a calculated manner.

Suicide takes a huge toll on people and the lives around them. Family, friends, and those close to an individual, all can offer support and words of encouragement to a person in distress. We all have the ability to positively impact the lives around us and demonstrate all the good that life has to offer.

Support groups, counseling, and medical attention; these are all alternatives we can provide as options. Yet despite all our efforts, one may still make that ultimate decision. For those individuals, clinics should offer unobtrusive and safe methods. Procedures such as medical injection should be made available. Or perhaps the body could be donated to science so the life does not die in vein. There are many other options few and far between that can be made available, but it should be up to the system and the States to decide how to implement these choices.

In the end, there needs to be well-established rules to govern any sort of process that enables this action. The survival of our ideals depends on the freedom of choice, yet a restriction on the choice to die seems counter intuitive. Every circumstance is different, and we all have our own reasons for making choices.

These are personal choices, ones that

ultimately society may not be able to influence. No law can physically prevent an individual from taking action. We can do our best to encourage moral behavior, but certain choices cannot be taken away.

However, to continue to treat suicide as taboo serves no justice and merely prolongs the pain and suffering. Only if we can take this topic seriously, and provide options to those in trouble, then can we prevent more lives from being tragically lost.

But to those individuals whom are troubled and feel like they are up against a wall, we owe it to them to offer our full support to help pick them back up. Life has so much to offer; sometimes all it takes is the right nudge to get back on track. Family, friends, and society can all act together to provide this help. There is nothing more tragic than the untimely decision one makes to end their own life.

*As Erica turned to leave the clinic, the nurse spoke up, 'Hang in there buddy'. This brought a smile to her face, one that had not been then in a long time. Erica now had something to look forward to, a new life, one where she had freedom and options.* ***A choice for happiness.***

## NOTES

---

*Would you end your life to save a strangers?*

# Peace of War

*Our defense is in the preservation of the spirit which prizes liberty as a heritage of all men, in all lands, everywhere.*

-President Abraham Lincoln

American past-times have the ability to transcend generations and bond communities together. They allow us to relate to different scenarios by drawing on a common language or experience. It is because of this that our Defensive Military strategy can be summed up in one short phrase: *Offense wins games, but defense wins championships.*

Having trust and reliance on our defensive strategy allows us to progress forward with confidence. It enables us to expand our abilities and raise the quality of life. A trusting defense provides us with a peace of mind and allows us to enjoy the pleasures in life.

A good defense is one that is well prepared for various scenarios and different attacks. A bad defense is always on it's heals, scrambling around and barely hanging in there. As a nation, we have a fairly advanced Defensive Military. Over the past 70 years, there have been only two major attacks on U.S. soil. This is no doubt due to the effort put forth by our defensive strategy.

But, as we prepare for the challenges that lie ahead, we must evaluate and ensure that our current strategy will protect us in the 21st century. We will start by defining the competition we are in; only then can we effectively plan out our defense knowing the likely scenarios we will face.

Looking forward, it is estimated we will achieve energy independence as a country sometime in the next 20 years. We are already self-sufficient in producing our own food; in 2014 we exported $149Billion worth. And with the advancements in robotics and meta-materials, we may soon be manufacturing all our own goods locally.

With our needs and necessities reassured over the next decade, what challenges do we have left to face as a nation? The answer is what has kept us in perpetual wars for 5 scores: **a protector of human rights and an enforcer of common equality.**

As a nation, we have torn down abusive regimes and eliminated national threats, but we also created more individual enemies. We must now be cautious of attacks by lone-wolfs and foreign militias. While we refuse to live in fear, we will be forced to take precautions to provide safety. And we must be able to trust each other, rather we will be trapped into a spy game and never advance.

The transition in our defensive strategy for the next century, must be gradual and well thought out. The process will require various steps each focusing on a different aspect of preventing conflict and defending our nation. This may require developing technologies and new techniques, but we as a nation have always been up for the task.

America has made strides over the past decades in the manufacturing and energy industries. However we continue to lack in producing the raw materials needed to source our innovations. To complicate matters, we have grown overly dependent on the Asian markets to fill this gap. We must put forth the effort to ensure the supply chain of raw materials is well distributed so we are not entirely dependent on one region of the world.

But, in order to determine how and what to diversify, we must take a thorough inventory of our capabilities. What goods and services are we capable of producing? How strong are we intellectually? Is our workforce growing, and in what sectors? Determining our current strength and abilities will allow us to set goals and become more self-reliant.

However, to realize our full potential, we must finally secure our borders and control what comes in and what leaves this country. This includes physical goods at our ports, information through digital channels, and people via immigration. We must document and account for all people and items that have been smuggled into our country. Understanding our land, our country, and what currently occupies it, should become a top priority in improving our defensive strategy.

It must be clear however, that in becoming a self-reliant nation, we do not transition to isolationism. World War II and the attacks on Pearl Harbor showed us that the longer we ignore the world's conflicts the harsher it becomes when we are ultimately brought in. By creating competitive trade agreements, and setting fair and reasonable prices, we can ensure friendly interactions with developed nations. And if our military force is required to intervene where human abuses are taking place, then we must strive towards economic prosperity as part of the peace process.

Additionally, we must clarify the interaction between our federal and local government when it comes to our defensive strategy. Our federal efforts and the U.S. Military should continue to protect us from international attacks. This includes not only physical attacks from around the world, but also the cyber and biological attacks that may slip across our border.

We will also rely on the federal government to organize and coordinate the local effort within our communities. There, we will rely on the State police as well as the good samaritan to monitor potential hazards. The importance of **See Something, Say Something** cannot be understated.

Ultimately becoming self-reliant will be a vast undertaking in transitioning our defensive strategy. Taking inventory of our abilities and securing our borders will only enhance our capabilities and allow us to gain confidence in ourselves as a nation. If we can align and coordinate our efforts to ensure our safety, one day we may be able to scale back our military force and focus more on peaceful advances.

# NOTES

*It's 4th and goal and we are down 3. Clock is ticking...*

# America's Family

*'Remember, remember always, that all of us, and you and I especially, are descended from immigrants and revolutionists.*

-President Franklin D. Roosevelt

$S$*traight off the boat.* It's a term our ancestors used to describe their arrival to this wonderful country in the 19th century. Having struggled through the American Revolution, and formulated a strong foundation in our Constitution, we opened our doors to those striving for a new beginning. America became known to the rest of the world as **The Land of Opportunity**. Soon the American Dream was born; if you worked hard and lived an honest life, you could provide for your family and open new doors for future generations.

But the world has changed since Lady Liberty welcomed those boats past Ellis Island. The danger to us no longer comes from military nations, but rather from individuals whom have crossed into our borders. We can no longer freely allow anyone into our country; the threats have worsened and the burden is greater.

Despite these changes, we still remain the land of opportunity. Students from around the world travel to America with visas in hand ready to attend universities. Dreams are still born in garages, and new businesses are opened daily. Unfortunately, the line to get into this country has never been longer, and the challenges to become an American citizen never more difficult. Further, the amount of undocumented workers, and those illegally here have taken such a toll on our system, that we no longer can provide basic reassurances to ourselves.

**We need to make citizenship and immigration a**

**top priority.** We can no longer pretend that those here illegally do no exist within our system. We need to welcome those willing to work hard and contribute honestly to the American system, and stop rejecting those who seek refuge from their own battered nations. We should be honored to provide the same opportunity and American Dream that our ancestors got. We are privileged to be able to continue the legacy of our immigration nation.

But, in order to recreate the successful system this country once had, we must clean up the mess our immigration system has become. We must take responsibility for those we have allowed into this country illegally and permitted to stay here. We need to prevent parents who travel here with the only intention of giving birth to an American baby. We must reward those who are willing to work hard and struggle for the American Dream.

To start, we will define those within our borders as either a citizen or a resident. A citizen is American by nature and is already accounted for within our system. Citizens pay taxes and contribute to society; they receive benefits and are provided protection. Residents on the other hand are also accounted for, but merely live in this country. They do not receive the same benefits and security that a full citizen does nor do they have the right to vote.

Being an American has its rewards and benefits; just because you live in the USA does not mean you are entitled to them. This is the main difference between a citizen and a resident.

With these two categories defined, we have purposely left out people who have snuck into our country. Whether we provide amnesty to residency, or a clear path to citizenship, it needs to become a top priority that we document and account for everyone within our borders. However, we should **not** expel people merely because we were ineffective in preventing their entry. Not everyone that resides or comes to our county needs to become a citizen right away, but they do need to be documented.

Once we have done a sufficient job in preventing illegal entry and amnesty is closed, then can we transition to full accountability within our borders. Only then can we expel or imprison those who are illegally in our country.

There are many within our borders whom are hard workers, respectful citizens, and contribute greatly to our country. But there are also those who are nothing more than a drain our system and a burden to the rest of us. Our social safety net has caught them and given little to no incentive for them to climb out. To these people, and the criminals some of you have become, you are not welcome here. Being American is about working hard, fulfilling dreams, and helping each other when times get tough. It is more than just a certificate or the location of your birth.

If we are to continue our nation's legacy, and provide the American Dream to our future generations, we need to get serious about immigration and hold those already here more accountable. While a population exists who have snuck into this country illegally, we certainly have not made it easy for them to become registered.

We as Americans need to think back to our roots and our ancestors that built this country. Born an immigration nation, we welcomed those who were willing to work hard and contribute to society. We provided an opportunity to those who arrived and watched as they transformed their dreams into reality.

But our nation has changed since our country's inception and so must the system that welcomes others. We must take into account the changes in the world since our nation's birth and the responsibility that comes with being in this country.

So, to those that value hard work and determination; to those that can dream and want a better life for their children; to those that are honest and loving, regardless of skin color, sexual orientation or origin of blood; to those that are American in every single way: *Welcome to the family.*

## NOTES

*Family is family is family...*

PERHAPS the sentiments contained in the following pages, are not *yet* sufficiently fashionable to procure them general favor; a long habit of not thinking a thing *wrong*, gives it a superficial appearance of being *right*, and raises at first a formidable outcry in defence of custom. But tumult soon subsides. Time makes more converts than reason. ¶ The cause of America is in a great measure the cause of all mankind. Many circumstances hath, and will arise, which are not local, but universal, and through which the principles of all Lovers of Mankind are affected, and in the Event of which, their Affections are interested. The laying a Country desolate with Fire and Sword, declaring War against the natural rights of all Mankind, and extirpating the Defenders thereof from the Face of the Earth, is the Concern of every Man to whom Nature hath given the Power of feeling; of which Class, regardless of Party Censure, is the AUTHOR ¶ Who the Author of this Production is, is wholly unnecessary to the Public, as the Object for Attention is the *Doctrine itself*, not the *Man*. Yet it may not be unnecessary to say, That he is unconnected with any Party, and under no sort of Influence public or private, but the influence of reason and principle. ¶ OF THE ORIGIN AND DESIGN OF GOVERNMENT IN GENERAL. ¶ SOME writers have so confounded society with government, as to leave little or no distinction between them; whereas they are not only different, but have different origins. Society is produced by our wants, and government by our wickedness; the former promotes our happiness *positively* by uniting our affections, the latter *negatively* by restraining our vices. The one encourages intercourse, the other creates distinctions. The first is a patron, the last a punisher. ¶ Society in every state is a blessing, but government even in its best state is but a necessary evil; in its worst state an intolerable one; for when we suffer, or are exposed to the same miseries *by a government*, which we might expect in a country *without government*, our calamity is heightened by reflecting that we furnish the means by which we suffer. Government, like dress, is the badge of lost innocence; the palaces of kings are built on the ruins of the bowers of paradise. For were the impulses of conscience clear, uniform, and irresistibly obeyed, man would need no other lawgiver; but that not being the case, he finds it necessary to surrender up a part of his property to furnish means for the protection of the rest; and this he is induced to do by the same prudence which in every other case advises him out of two evils to choose the least. *Wherefore*, security being the true design and end of government, it unanswerably follows that whatever *form* thereof appears most likely to ensure it to us, with the least expense and greatest benefit, is preferable to all others. ¶ In order to gain a clear and just idea of the design and end of government, let us suppose a small number of persons settled in some sequestered part of the earth, unconnected with the rest, they will then represent the first peopling of any country, or of the world. In this state of natural liberty, society will be their first thought. A thousand motives will excite them thereto, the strength of one man is so unequal to his wants, and his mind so unfitted for perpetual solitude, that he is soon obliged to seek assistance and relief of another, who in his turn requires the same. Four or five united would be able to raise a tolerable dwelling in the midst of a wilderness, but *one* man might labour out the common period of life without accomplishing any thing; when he had felled his timber he could not remove it, nor erect it after it was removed; hunger in the mean time would urge him from his work, and every different want call him a different way. Disease, nay even misfortune would be death, for though neither might be mortal, yet either would disable him from living, and reduce him to a state in which he might rather be said to perish than to die. ¶ Thus necessity, like a gravitating power, would soon form our newly arrived emigrants into society, the reciprocal blessings of which, would supersede, and render the obligations of law and government unnecessary while they remained perfectly just to each other; but as nothing but heaven is impregnable to vice, it will unavoidably happen, that in proportion as they surmount the first difficulties of emigration, which bound them together in a common cause, they will begin to relax in their duty and attachment to each other; and this remissness, will point out the necessity, of establishing some form of government to supply the defect of moral virtue. ¶ Some convenient tree will afford them a State-House, under the branches of which, the whole colony may assemble to deliberate on public matters. It is more than probable that their first laws will have the title only of REGULATIONS, and be enforced by no other penalty than public disesteem. In this first parliament every man, by natural right, will have a seat. ¶ But as the colony increases, the public concerns will increase likewise, and the distance at which the members may be separated, will render it too inconvenient for all of them to meet on every occasion as at first, when their number was small, their habitations near, and the public concerns few and trifling. This will point out the convenience of their consenting to leave the legislative part to be managed by a select number chosen from the whole body, who are supposed to have the same concerns at stake which those have who appointed them, and who will act in the same manner as the whole body would act were they present. If the colony continue increasing, it will become necessary to augment the number of the representatives, and that the interest of every part of the colony may be attended to, it will be found best to divide the whole into convenient parts, each part sending its proper number; and that the *elected* might never form to themselves an interest separate from the *electors*, prudence will point out the propriety of having elections often; because as the *elected* might by that means return and mix again with the general body of the *electors* in a few months, their fidelity to the public will be secured by the prudent reflection of not making a rod for themselves. And as this frequent interchange will establish a common interest with every part of the community, they will mutually and naturally support each other, and on this (not on the unmeaning name of king) depends the *strength of government, and the happiness of the governed.* ¶ Here then is the origin and rise of government; namely, a mode rendered necessary by the inability of moral virtue to govern the world; here too is the design and end of government, viz. freedom and security. And however our eyes may be dazzled with show, or our ears deceived by sound; however prejudice may warp our wills, or interest darken our understanding, the simple voice of nature and of reason will say, it is right. ¶ MANKIND being originally equals in the order of creation, the equality could only be destroyed by some subsequent circumstance; the distinctions of rich, and poor, may in a great measure be accounted for, and that without having recourse to the harsh ill- sounding names of oppression and avarice. Oppression is often the *consequence*, but seldom or never the *means* of riches; and though avarice will preserve a man from being necessitously poor, it generally makes him too timorous to be wealthy. ¶ THOUGHTS ON THE PRESENT STATE OF AMERICAN AFFAIRS. ¶ IN the following pages I offer nothing more than simple facts, plain arguments, and common sense; and have no other preliminaries to settle with the reader, than that he will divest himself of prejudice and prepossession, and suffer his reason and his feelings to determine for themselves; that he will put *on*, or rather that he will not put *off*, the true character of a man, and generously enlarge his views beyond the present day.... This is not inflaming or exaggerating matters, but trying them by those feelings and affections which nature justifies, and without which, we should be incapable of discharging the social duties of life, or enjoying the felicities of it. I mean not to exhibit horror for the purpose of provoking revenge, but to awaken us from fatal and unmanly slumbers, that we may pursue determinately some fixed object. It is not in the power of Britain or of Europe to conquer America, if she do not conquer herself by *delay* and *timidity*. The present winter is worth an age if rightly employed, but if lost or neglected, the whole continent will partake of the misfortune; and there is no punishment which that man will not deserve, be he who, or what, or where he will, that may be the means of sacrificing a season so precious and useful.... Every quiet method for peace hath been ineffectual. Our prayers have been rejected with disdain; and only tended to convince us, that nothing flatters vanity, or confirms obstinacy in kings more than repeated petitioning -- and nothing hath contributed more than that very measure to make the Kings of Europe absolute: Witness Denmark and Sweden. Wherefore, since nothing but blows will do, for God's sake, let us come to a final separation, and not leave the next generation to be cutting throats, under the violated unmeaning names of parent and child.... The colonies have manifested such a spirit of good order and obedience to continental government, as is sufficient to make every reasonable person easy and happy on that head. No man can assign the least pretence for his fears, on any other grounds, than such as are truly childish and ridiculous, viz. that one colony will be striving for superiority over another.... A government of our own is our natural right: And when a man seriously reflects on the precariousness of human affairs, he will become convinced, that it is infinitely wiser and safer, to form a constitution of our own in a cool deliberate manner, while we have it in our power, than to trust such an interesting event to time and chance. If we omit it now, some Massanello* may hereafter arise, who laying hold of popular disquietudes, may collect together the desperate and the discontented, and by assuming to themselves the powers of government, may sweep away the liberties of the continent like a deluge.... O ye that love mankind! Ye that dare oppose, not only the tyranny, but the tyrant, stand forth! ¶ OF THE PRESENT ABILITY OF AMERICA  ¶ It is not in numbers, but in unity, that our great strength lies; yet our present numbers are sufficient to repel the force of all the world. The Continent hath, at this time, the largest body of armed and disciplined men of any power under Heaven; and is just arrived at that pitch of strength, in which, no single colony is able to support itself, and the whole, when united, can accomplish the fact, and either more, or, less than this, might be fatal in its effects. ¶ APPENDIX ¶ The present state of America is truly alarming to every man who is capable of reflexion. Without law, without government, without any other mode of power than what is founded on, and granted by courtesy. Held together by an unexampled concurrence of sentiment, which, is nevertheless subject to change, and which, every secret enemy is endeavoring to dissolve. Our present condition, is, Legislation without law; wisdom without a plan; a constitution without a name; and, what is strangely astonishing, perfect Independence contending for dependance. The instance is without a precedent; the case never existed before; and who can tell what may be the event? The property of no man is secure in the present unbraced system of things. The mind of the multitude is left at random, and seeling no fixed object before them, they pursue such as fancy or opinion starts. Nothing is criminal; there is no such thing as treason; wherefore, every one thinks himself at liberty to act as he pleases.... On these grounds I rest the matter. And as no offer hath yet been made to refute the doctrine contained in the former editions of this pamphlet, it is a negative proof, that either the doctrine cannot be refuted, or, that the party in favor of it are too numerous to be opposed. WHEREFORE, instead of gazing at each other with suspicious or doubtful curiosity, let each of us, hold out to his neighbor the hearty hand of friendship, and unite in drawing a line, which, like an act of oblivion shall bury in forgetfulness every former dissention. Let the names of Whig and Tory be extinct; and let none other be heard among us, than those of *a good citizen, an open and resolute friend, and a virtuous supporter of the* RIGHTS *of* MANKIND *and of the* FREE AND INDEPENDENT STATES OF AMERICA.

*Excerpts taken from*
COMMON SENSE
Thomas Paine
Published in 1776

# NOTES

# I, Voter

*The vote is the most powerful instrument ever devised by man
for breaking down injustice and destroying the terrible walls
which imprison men because they are different from other men.*

-President Lyndon B. Johnson

In order to form a more perfect union, we the people govern ourselves. Democracy helps protect society from tyranny and unjust law; voting gives power to the people.

Today however, the reality of the representation system and our voter laws make us feel powerless. Our democracy is failing in essential ways: casting votes, and the selection of qualified leaders to represent us.

Intrinsically, the voting process requires improvements, but we cannot ignore the issue of an ignorant majority. This is the principle behind the Electoral College and weighing each state differently; every vote is not represented equally. Our discussion focuses first on the voting system itself followed by suggestions to strengthen our voting democracy.

The voting booth represents a sacred idea that our selection counts towards an equal part in making a self-governing choice. Suspicions rise however once that ballot enters the box. Do ballots get lost and how do we ensure the vote reaches the actual candidate? The current system is lacking not only in transparency, but checks and balances in the vote itself.

Understandably however, the anonymity currently provided to us is something we cannot afford to give up. In essence, voting in privacy is just as important as the vote it self. This protects us from outside pressure, and allows us to vote as a true individual. To take away that privacy, would be to weaken the strength of the vote.

A modern vote requires verifiability and anonymity in a new voting democracy. It also seems logical to add transparency wherever possible. We as a people demand a fair voting process.

One enhancement, for example, could provide us with a receipt as we submit our vote. Once all the ballots are tabulated, the individual results are made public, either online or distributed locally. As voters, we can than verify our selection through information on the receipt. This creates a verified ballot, and reduces fraud by authenticating votes. Anonymity is maintained by requiring a unique one-time login and a two-form factor authentication.

Additionally, one should be required to identify themselves prior to voting. Identification ensures the proper American obtains a ballot and only votes once. Conversely it is just as logical to allow citizens to register to vote at the ballot box. The barrier for Americans to legally vote should be as low as possible.

To strength democracy even further the ballot box should be open for at least a 36-hour period across the country. This will also help mitigate concerns about time zone differences and exit polls swaying the later vote. Make no mistake; there is a difference between voting independently and knowing the current results while voting.

Now to address the gorilla in the room: the ignorant, uneducated voter. This individual does not know the issues and has not spent the time to learn the long-term implications of decisions being made. These voters are easily manipulated, superfluous, and impervious to fact. Individually, they are stand up citizens, contributing hard to achieve their American dream. Collectively, put together they can lead to destructive decisions.

The question then, is how do we protect society and our institutions from the harm of a short-sited majority? The popular majority will not always select the best solution, while taking into account a wide range of considerations. The majority may pursue short-term fulfillment rather than long-term sustainability. However it is our obligation as a society, to prepare for the future and maintain our greatness.

To address this concern, we could allow voters to recall representatives across the nation. The burden to recall will be high, but this would enable the conscience voter to provide a balance to populist movements. In the end, the truth will win.

Ultimately, democracy must provide fair representation of differing opinions. There is a thin line between authoritarian rule and protecting society from poor decisions. We cannot allow the powerful to overpower and control the majority.

This is why voting is of the uttermost importance. It gives each individual an opportunity to contribute and make decisions as to the future of our nation. But it is also a tool that can be abused, susceptible to fraud, and not always accurate. History is full of examples where the majority has made unforgivable choices, such as the support of Nazism in

Germany, or the propagation of the slave trade in America.

Similarly, if there is no confidence in an individual vote, then the system of democracy will fail. Lack of confidence leads to low voter turnout and a disenfranchised population. Once the spotlight on democracy is removed, accountability is lost and the system becomes strive with corruption.

**To vote** is our constitutional power and the privilege that beholds us to ensure our representatives act as honest individuals. Voting is the foundation of democracy, but our system needs maintenance since the 250 years ago it was created. Through neglect, we have allowed the integrity of the ballot to diminish over time. Only as a collective society and an individual voter, can we enforce change. By increasing ballot security, and adding verifiably to the voting system, we can we begin the first step in strengthening America's democracy.

## NOTES

*VOTE!*

# SUMMER

# E.D.U.

*Education is what remains after one has forgotten what one has learned in school.*

-Albert Einstein

*When Erica was 16, Congress passed the highly contested SEDU Act and by the following summer, she was enrolled in one of the nation's first Summer Education programs. She tried to resist going, but since her parents refused to sign the waiver, she didn't have much choice. What started as hesitant turned into a summer filled with fun, learning, making new friends; she even had her first summer fling. It was a summer she would never forget.*

Our culture of closing school during the summer creates a missed opportunity for our nation and needs to be reevaluated. We let down our future generations when we do not approach education seriously. We can no longer afford to let our kid's education falter during the summer months.

Rather than increase classroom time however, we should look to supplement our traditional educational system and sustain learning throughout the summer. We need our children to learn how to co-operate better and solve problems as a team. The programs should put an emphasis on filling in the gaps of classroom learning: financial advice, life planning, technical skills, etc.

These proposed summer programs would be multipurpose: to sustain and supplement our children's education, and perhaps more importantly better integrate our children through cooperative activities. This will also provide an opportunity to reinforce social responsibility. We must strive to provide an environment where our kids can learn team cooperation and be collaborative. Raising our children to be tolerant will guarantee the prosperity of our nation.

Therefore it is imperative that we address the serious divide within our country, and not wait for the next tragedy to unite us. Long-term solutions will be developed with the next generation as they mold into our society. No better opportunity exists to sustain education and provide team-building skills than the currently neglected time during the summer. Our traditional education system requires a system of checks and balances.

On that note, learning aspects should focus on providing a benchmark to evaluate a student's progress. There can also be an opportunity to prepare and provide background for the upcoming school year. To optimize the traditional learning experience, we should encourage our kids to verify material and prepare for the upcoming school year.

At the beginning of each school year, valuable time is wasted reviewing previously taught material. This is an unfair burden we place on our teachers and education system. Our students do not need more time in the classroom; rather we need to better optimize their time already spent there.

To supplement to our education system however, without considering the costs would be irresponsible; and these summer programs should be anything but. Consequently, existing infrastructure can be used to facilitate these programs, such as a vacant high schools or old military bases. However in the event that facilities do need to be built, they should be designed as multi-purpose and at a moments notice convert into a military base, refugee camp, or natural disaster relief center. If we plan according, the cost of creating multi-purpose disaster relief centers can be absorbed across agencies.

Additionally, to better-integrate society, we must develop these summer programs nationally. Incentives will allure students to attend programs out of state in neighborhoods they might not otherwise be exposed to. This will ensure future generations are exposed to the different living experiences that make up our country.

Further, each summer program will be based on a regional curriculum. For example, programs out in California might be more technical based, while those in Iowa would be more agricultural based. In doing so, the people of the state or region are given incentive to share knowledge and skills with the rest of our nation. The federal government can provide incentive for each state to educate students from across the country with a regionalized trade set and encourage diversity. A failure to harvest the collective differences in our country and spread acquired knowledge would be a waste of the dynamics that make our country. We need to grow strong together, not individually strong.

A fair criticism of these proposed summer programs centers around the loss of current opportunities: family travel, summer camp, and jobs. Is it prudent to interfere with the current life learning opportunities? Therefore, summer programs should be optional, though highly encouraged. It would be a shame to forgo a vast development opportunity, but nonetheless, like the traditional classroom, we cannot force schooling. However, there must be accountability if the parents decide to withhold their child from education summer programs.

Any summer program, whether it is provided by the state, or through private organizations, should focus on sustaining education while ensuring co-operative skills development. By utilizing existing infrastructure and providing sustainable jobs, we benefit both ourselves, and future generations. Summer is a time filled with joy; we should make sure our future is too.

*By the end of the summer, Erica had created her own app, installed a kitchen sink, and discovered the true meaning of friendship. And although her romance was only a summer fling, deep down she knew there would be a future if she tried.*

## NOTES

---

*What is your fondest memory growing up in the summer?*

# Earth To America

*America is never wholly herself unless she is engaged in high moral principle. We as a people have such a purpose today. It is to make kinder the face of the nation and gentler the face of the world.*

-President George H. W. Bush

When you are on top, everything goes well: the sun is shining, people ask you for advice, and even the birds sing you a tune. But beware, others are clawing to take your spot and root for your failure. This competition is good, it keeps you focused and sharp; helps you appreciate the luxuries of being on top.

America is on top; we have been for close to a century. Collectively as a nation, we have fulfilled the America Dream. From the beginning, we've been an ambitious nation with vast opportunity in front of us. The world however has gotten a lot smaller since we've become a dominant leader. With that comes responsibility, not just to us, but also to all the people of the world.

Ultimately, at the top, we run the risk of complacently. Here, it is easy to become lazy, vain, and self-absorbed. Over time we tend to forget the sacrifices made and become ignorant of the problems of those who did not make it. In order to maintain our position of strength, we must apply the same effort that led to our greatness. It is not just a responsibility; it is essential.

Our role as a country has varied throughout history. We earned our leadership, through hard work and sacrifice, not just of capital but of human spirit as well. We have grown during this process and defined our global role. It is up to all of us, right now, to seize the moment and redefine our role in the world, before the world defines ours.

Currently, the world is going through changes, possibly on the brink of monumental. The 21st century was born on the cusp of the technical revolution; never before has change occurred at a faster pace. Those that adapt will succeed, while those who are uncompromising will break.

America is no exception; the Great Recession irreparably changed us, splintering a divide within our country. Now more than ever, we must outline our true values and plan for the future. As change approaches us, it is imperative to provide goals and a clear direction for not just our future, but the globe's as well; it is the responsibility of the world's leader to do so. Therefor, submitted to you is a draft of America's 21st century doctrine:

*We Pledge as Americans, to fulfill the legacy of our founding fathers and promote peace, health, and prosperity to all. We recognize that all inhabitants of this earth have an equal right to exist and live free from persecution. To those who blatantly ignore human rights, and challenge our values, may you be foolish enough to deserve the wrath of our might. A crime against one is a crime against all humanity; we will not tolerate it. Success has bore us the responsibility to be defenders of democracy, a protector of human rights and an enforcer of common equality. We shall protect and defend not just ourselves, but those in need, from the tyranny of evil that forcefully impose their will on others. We shall work to ensure that every life is granted safety and access to the recognition and rights that every human deserves: freedom, equality, justice, and privacy. We hereby decree these human liberties for all.*

Unfortunately at times in our history we have gone against these morals and subsequently, humanity has paid a price. The harm we have inflicted upon ourselves could have been prevented if we remained true to our core values.

In the 1940s, we were late to enter WWII and the events of Pearl Harbor proved we cannot abstain from world atrocities. We failed as a nation to stand up to world obscenity and as a result millions were executed.

At other times, we used force when other means could have been utilized. The Vietnam and Iraq wars demonstrated that not every conflict demands force, and heavy hitting can create unintended consequences and new enemies. We must strive to help and protect those in harm's way in a more productive manner.

For example, our nation has successfully employed economic sanctions to control and influence other countries with a forceful military to deter violations. The broader implications of using force must always be considered when activating our military.

Sanctions however only work if the global community is willing to act in unison. Cooperation will only occur if we remain friendly and treat other nations with respect; projecting fairness and equality maintains our position as a world leader. We must work with other nations who share common interests and support our doctrine- only then can we ensure the safety of the world and ourselves.

The changes in the 21<sup>st</sup> century that lie ahead will effect alliances and governing powers. In order to minimize damage from these changes, we must strive towards self-reliance and energy independence. Our global supply chain needs to become diversified so we can adjust to the continuing fluctuations. As a nation we must strive for that balance between integration and independence.

**Change is upon us.** It is up to us to grab it and make the most of the opportunity, this is the American way. We must continue to promote the ideals that made us great, and define our new role in the 21st century. Together, as a nation of immigrants, we must help mold the future of humanity.

## NOTES

*We, as a United Nation, stand for…*

# Next Up

*I am vice president. In this I am nothing, but I may be everything.*

-President John Adams

The Vice President of the United States is the next in line to lead our country in the event of tragedy. In times of deep despair and mourning, we will look to this person to guide us out of darkness and heal as a nation. Once sworn in, he or she will assume power over the world's strongest military with nuclear capabilities. There is only one American, whom if tragedy should strike, can become the world's most powerful person. **This is our Vice President.**

Fortunately, this has only happened twice in our county's history, each without dire consequences. However if we take a look at the role of the Vice President, we actually see a decline in responsibility. In fact, the Vice President has become more of a consultant; always being assigned tasks, but never given the authority.

The Vice President's role has become one of the most under utilized positions in federal government. The constitution grants very little responsibility for our nation's second in command: a duty to resolve deadlock in the event of a congressional tie.

The constitution defines our expectations of the Vice President. As next in line, he or she must be able to perform every required task of the President, but with little experience or practice. We ask a lot of the Vice President without providing adequate preparation.

As a nation, it is imperative that we clearly define the role of the Vice President. We must ensure they are fully prepared and qualified to run this country, going above and beyond with preparation because ultimately they will lack Presidential experience.

Being one step removed from the President enables the Vice President to realize the full impact of the decisions made. He or she should be aware of more details of the day-to-day operations of this country than the President. Only there can one see the direct impact decisions have at the top.

Being privy to the minute details of how our country runs will not only prepare the Vice President for the next position, but it will also produce a more efficient government. As stipulated by our Constitution, the role of the Vice President is to act as presiding officer of the Senate and cast a vote in the event of stalemate. Given the current gridlock, this responsibility presents a vast opportunity for one person to greatly impact our government.

The current dysfunction in Washington is self-inflected harm. Our ineffective Congressional branch has slowed down our economy with their inability to make decisions. The inaction, constant bickering, and unwillingness to compromise have caused irreparable harm to our country. Drastic action must be taken in order to save us from ourselves.

To eradicate the gridlock within Washington, we must seize this opportunity and create a position that redefines the role of the Vice President. We must enable and then demand that our Vice President keeps Congress running. Being privy to the inner working of our government, the Vice President is in a unique role to move things along. He or she will be able to provide the missing details that congress needs in order to make decisions and move this country forward. We will continue to regress if we fail to act.

The gridlock in Washington however extends far beyond just Congress, and therefore so should the responsibilities of the Vice President. He or she will be able to oversee the government from a unique position where the coordination of various branches of government can be smoothly integrated. Currently, many branches operate in silos, communicating very little with other facilities of government. The Vice President should be aware of all the efforts going on and help facilitate synergy. In turn, this will provide knowledge of the federal government's inner workings to the Vice President.

Ultimately, our country demands vast self-improvement. By redefining the responsibilities of the Vice President, we are providing that power to the second in command through awareness. Being responsible for ensuring our country operates smoothly will uniquely qualify them for the next role.

Currently, the Vice President is an after thought; a person who is tied to a Presidential candidate. The position of the Vice President deserves a better-defined vetting process. Clearly, the role is just as, if not more, important than the President, and should no longer be treated as merely a running mate. We should expect the Vice President to work in tandem with the President in order to accomplish the best for our country.

To our advantage, the Vice President is able to work behind the scenes because the spotlight of leadership is on the President of our nation. This will re-delegate the responsibilities of the White House so our President can lead the country, while our Vice President helps run the country. The Vice President is in a distinct position to remove the crippling gridlock of our government, and subsequently the role must be re-evaluated.

Perhaps this is what our country needs; a sole dedication to getting our elected officials to cooperate and work together. Whether is it is ensuring Congress functions, or redundancies in government are removed, the Vice President needs to step up and take care of what is broken from the inside. The second in command is in the best position to assume this role and make our country function again.

# NOTES

*Who is your Vice President?*

# Spicy Blue

*Upon reproduction, it is estimated that only one in one million copies will have the right hue of blue to reflect Spicy Blue. Even then, the light has to hit the paper just right for the color to be seen.*

My favorite color is spicy blue. It is a rarity in of itself, only seen in certain circumstances. I first discovered it one evening when there wasn't a cloud in the sky and the sun was about to set, leaving a crisp blue aurora. At that moment, the sky sparkled, as if trying to shine. Ever since then I've been on the search to find spicy blue again.

The rarity of spicy blue makes it all the more special. I know there is no one else out there with the same favorite color. When I do see it, it becomes an exciting moment; perhaps I am the only one with the eyes who can see it!

There are, however, other exotic colors out there. Mother nature provides a plethora of colors like crisp orange, sour purple, and cold white. In fact, I once had a friend whose favorite color was clear; that was neat to see. Last I heard, she now prefers soft green.

Of course any color can be a favorite color, as some might prefer the vibrant yellow, while others might stick with the dependable red. Pink has made resurgence as of late and is convincingly popular. The possibilities for color are infinite, allowing everyone a chance to discover their own favorite.

For me, spicy blue induces excitement; this is why it is my favorite color. Others have different reasons why their color is preferred; that is the basis for personal preference. Selecting a favorite color represents a unique opportunity to make an unbiased selection of no significant consequence. There are zero repercussions for changing your mind; no judgment for the haphazard reasoning or selection. It is your favorite color, a personal preference no one can influence or take away.

Even if color isn't your favorite thing, everyone one can relate to having a favorite something. Perhaps you have a favorite sports team, or preference for a particular food. You might have a favorite song or even a favorite television show. These all are a personal preference, something we get to choose. No one can tell us what our favorite color is, that would be absurd to comprehend.

For the purposes of this discussion, having a favorite color represents individuality and freedom. A favorite choice strikes right down to the core and defines whom we are. No matter what label society has given us, whether it is white or black, gay or straight, we all have the right to choose our own favorite color. So go wild with your selection, be unique. No one can ever take this away from you; **this is your favorite color.**

Personal opinions, the freedom to choose and everything in between; these all are embraced by selecting a favorite color. Individuality is the fabric of America; it is what drove us here to colonize and the basis for our Constitution. Try as they might to suppress, no one can ever take away your opinion. As a country we should cherish the right to choose a favorite color as the individuality and citizenship it represents.

Even if you are abused, repressed, or neglected,

in your mind you always have the right to embrace a favorite color. This undeniable right exemplifies our instinct for freedom and singularity.

While personal preference is a basic human instinct, the right to choose and make personal decisions is not always protected. This was the basis for the Constitution and the founding of our country, but over the years, has not always been respected. Pregnancy prevention and end of life care are just a few of the personal decisions that has unfortunately become of governing power of the public opinion. Imagine, a public opinion determining your favorite color! When put into perspective, it seems ludicrous trying to control personal decisions.

The right to choose a favorite color invokes the passion of freedom and basic human liberties. Like the color wheel, individuality thrives when choices are infinite. This is the basis for creativity and originality, the spirit of our American Dream. America thrives when choices are plentiful and personal opinions embraced. We falter when we suppress ideas and limit potential. This is evident by the 50 states we have created, and the united country that has formed. We are at our strongest when we work together, our weakest when we strife. Respecting each other and personal opinions is the first step in ensuring a strong United States.

Choosing where to live or having a favorite town or city is a unique American experience that we often overlook. This freedom of residence promotes state individuality, allowing local communities to choose laws that shape and compliment the culture of the region. A mutual respect of these differences is required if America is to continue to succeed. Society crumbles when it becomes divided, blossoms if it remains united.

Embracing a favorite color is not only fun, but to the core, invaluable to American society. This sensation of freedom and unique individuality helps us all empathize with the right to choose and make personal decisions. Select a favorite color and wear it with pride; but be sure to respect those that choose differently.

In the end, I'm willing to share spicy blue. Sure, it is my favorite color, but I can't go around claiming no one else can enjoy it either. Spice blue is unique and special to me, I can only hope that your favorite color provides similar meaning. Perhaps you will enjoy all shades of green or maybe even the entire color wheel. Anything is possible; it is all our personal preference. Arguably, America's favorite color is red, white, and blue. What is yours?

## *NOTES*

*What is your favorite color?!*

# House Of
# GOD

*I think different religions are different doors to the same house.*

-Steve Jobs

Religious beliefs are not determined by the size of a surrounding community, but rather by the internal experiences we all bear witness to. Faith is a personal journey, and in order to truly embrace God, we must allow everybody to follow their own path. Community respect is the sacrifice we pay for personal serenity.

On the surface, it is quite easy to separate church and state; a government maintains society, while religion is directed at the personal and inner self. It is our individual self however that becomes entangled, occupying the boundary between church and state.

In the United States, we accept that others will practice different beliefs. America is a sanctuary for religious freedom, not a place for imposing crusades. This liberty permits all individuals to opt-out of any government program that infringes on one's personal beliefs.

Religious freedoms however are personal and therefor do not necessarily extend to organizations and companies. Our government has the authority to oversee companies so that they do not harm employees. This includes not only regulating a physically safe environment, but requiring a place where individuals are free from persecution for their beliefs and religion. No authority, whether it is government or private entity, has the privilege to deny faith and personal beliefs; that is not within human jurisdiction.

On the other hand, freedom to practice religion

does not extend to the realm of infinite possibilities. Religion beliefs do not permit one to abstain from their duties to contribute to household and society. We all have a moral obligation to subscribe to society and contribute in a positive manner. America is a social contract in which we have committed to each other the protection and safety for everyone to practice their own faith. This core, undeniable human right has laid the foundation for our country.

The United States was created out of necessity to ensure freedom for individuals to practice any religion or belief without fear of prosecution. America provides the tolerance and freedom to have a belief and participate in an organized religion.

*Treat on to others, as you would have done to you.* This is the Golden Rule of society, and a common theme throughout all religions. It is not *treat others the way they treat you* nor is it *treat yourself better than you treat others.* **Fairness must rule above all.** Treat others, the way you expect yourself to be treated.

Within American culture, the term **God** is unlike any other word in our language: universal definition for a religious belief in something greater than oneself, a commitment to a higher power. The term **God** and what it symbolizes, represents a deeply personal emotion; at all costs, this must be protected and sanctified for each individual.

Let there be no misunderstanding, faith among us transcends. **Allah, Christ, God**; these are all symbols that are meant to invoke a unique and personal sensation and have different meaning depending on your faith.

For some of us, our faith is grounded in religion, while others have faith that there is no natural order and everything is as such. But without faith, there is no will; without the will, there is no action; faith is a commonality we all share.

Whichever way you look at it, faith is a strong belief, it enables us to take that leap and evolve and grow. Regardless if personal experiences have proven otherwise, we must respect each other's personal choice; understand that we are all given different paths and will reach separate conclusions.

Faith is an undeniable human privilege and the most fundamental right to choose. We all have the ability to develop our own personal faith regardless of outside influence; we always have a choice, a decision starts with faith. No institution or person can ever limit or take faith away from us.

Above all, we must be tolerant and respectful of each other's faith. As a country, getting along and working as a united entity is key to survival. In order for America to remain strong, we must form a deeper appreciate for treating each other with respect. It is a sin to prevent an individual from connecting with his or her faith.

The United States of America is declared as a sanctuary for religious freedom. It was a key component in establishing our country and a basic building block in the foundation of our constitution. It is our moral obligation to perpetuate this ideal and provide sanctuary for those persecuted for their faith. The United States guarantees the freedom to practice religion without persecution and harm.

Through a deep understanding of what it means to be human, we establish that above all, faith is unique to an individual and an undeniable right to choose. Only when we respect each other, can we truly succeed as one. May God bless us, and may God bless the United States of America.

## NOTES

*What do you believe?*

# Re-investing In America

*Blessed are the young for they shall inherit the national debt.*

-President Herbert Hoover

America was founded on the back of those who sacrificed their well being in order to provide a better tomorrow for us, the next generation. When explorers first crossed the Atlantic, and settlers first moved out west, it was not for their immediate benefit. No, they did so for the future of their country. This expenditure of energy and physical sacrifice enabled our country to flourish while avoiding fiscal liability.

As the population grew and human capital became more abundant, national monetary systems expanded. Money helped quantify one physical good or service to another. This resulted in a vast expansion in the tradability of products, the growth and creation of a fiscal economy.

This paradigm shift however, also introduced the concept of debt, where one could borrow and spend more than they possessed. If carefully managed, debt and borrowing can be a productive tool in sustaining growth.

Run-away debt however will lead to an economic collapse affecting not just those whose borrowed unwisely, but those who acted responsible as well. An irresponsible borrower will damage not just his or her own finances, but everyone tied to the fiscal economy as well. As debt continues to rise, the point of inflection becomes greater and greater until it is too late to adjust.

It is imperative, not just for ourselves, but for future generations, that we check and balance our fiscal policy. Clearly, spending more than one takes in will lead to disaster; therefore we must ensure we spend wisely.

Unfortunately the accrued debt we carry from generation to generation is prohibitive to success. The American Dream we promise provides the prospect of a brighter future with growth. This is why spending and reinvesting in America needs to be a forefront issue of modern politics.

As we discuss America's fiscal policy, it becomes impossible to neglect the absolute role of government; it is not a business and nor should it act as one. However, the laws of debt and fiscal policy are universal and therefore the administration must be accountable.

America is a public institution, an entity in of itself. It falls in-between the realm of private business and non-profit charity. Our government cannot depend on taxes and charity to sustain itself and therefor must reduce cost. However, a government with surplus should be viewed just as poorly as an institution in debt; there must be a correct balance. A surplus reflects a lack of re-investment and a limiting a potential future. Therefore it is imperative to review America's fiscal policy and balance our budget.

To start, the government's yearly budget should not exceed the previous year's income. This statement seems self-evident, but for decades our budget has failed to do this. Annually, once taxes are collected, a fiscal report should be presented focusing on income and revenue. This will enable us to create a clear budget for the upcoming year.

Additionally, the budget should broken into different categories and presented to the public: military and security defense; roads, communications, and infrastructure; school and education; health and the well being of the American citizen, and finally debt and interest. If we force ourselves to simplify our spending and budget categories, we can plan and allocate our funds properly.

However reality and policy do not always coexist. Natural disasters, unforeseen events and external circumstances all demand that we spend more than we sometimes budget. Our government should be permitted to spend more than budgeted, however only under extraordinary circumstances.

The American public requires a concise budget and spending report, thus keeping in check a fiscally responsible government. It is our responsibility to future generations to pay off of our debt so they can indulge in the luxuries we take for granted today.

We must as a society invest not only in our country but also in the American citizen. A healthier, smarter citizen can give back to their country in a prosperous way. Lack of re-investment, especially at the state level, limits future potential. The American Dream produced visionaries like Albert Einstein, Steve Jobs, and Elon Musk. Therefor it is not only wise, but required, that America invest back into its citizens to ensure a brighter and prosperous future.

## NOTES

*What does the American Dream mean to you?*

# Liquid Haze

*First you take a drink, then the drink takes a drink, then the drink takes you.*

-F. Scott Fitzgerald

No matter which state you find yourself in, if you are under 21 and walk into a bar, they will not serve you. However, if you remember the 1950s, then you know a time when cigarettes where cool, not all cars had seatbelts, and people would buy and consume alcohol as early as 18. But that was then and times have changed.

In the 1980s when confronted with the historic rise of drunk driving and fatal car accidents, organizations like Mothers Against Drunk Driving put pressure on local and federal governments to step in and take action. Rightfully so, drunk driving was becoming became the leprosy of society.

However, the effects of prohibition still lingered and mandating a national minimum drinking age proved difficult. So in 1984, the National Minimum Drinking Age Act was passed, tying together federal highway funds to each state's minimum drinking age. Since then, drunk driving and accidental deaths on the road has decreased tremendously. This was a clear win for humanity; but did we infringe on a state's right to enact local laws? Today, if a state reduces their legal drinking age, they lose federal funding for maintaining highways and roads.

Additionally, the fact that the current drinking age is 21, yet the drafting age is 18, has not been lost on many. Until recently, one could be sent to war and return from battle still not being able to order a drink at the bar. There is irony in being asked to serve and protect our country while at the same time denying legal rights to consume alcohol.

However, there are many benefits to having an older drinking age. The sharp downfall in drunk driving incidents and the decrease in alcohol related deaths cannot be understated. Our country has a hazy history when it comes to laws pertaining to alcohol, so changes must exhibit caution and careful planning. We must commit to the progress we have made in mitigating preventable tragedy. To ensure we do not regress as a society when it comes to the consumption and possible abuse of alcohol, here are a few requirements:

First and foremost, alcohol needs to stay out of high schools, which encompasses students as young as 13. At this age, our children are very susceptible to peer pressure and at risk for making life-damaging decisions. Consumption of alcohol at a young age has been tied to stunted growth and a handicapped mind.

Second, providing or selling alcohol to minors should become taboo. We hold back our youth when we poison their mind with drugs and alcohol; therefore if caught selling or providing alcohol to minors, one's privilege to purchase alcohol should be revoked for a minimum of 5 years.

Finally, drunk-driving rates cannot not increase. This was the reasoning behind enacting a minimum drinking age of 21, and by all accounts, has been effective. We cannot permit this progress to be undone. Further, breathalyzer ignitions should be considered for those who are starting to drive and have legal access to alcohol. It is at this age that we need to reinforce the consequences of drinking and driving and teach proper responsibility.

Taking these requirements into consideration, it should be possible to lower the minimum drinking age without regression of society. For example, if we lowered the age to 19, we ensure, although not guarantee, that alcohol will continue to stay out of the high schools. It also creates a buffer for those learning to drive, by requiring a few years of driving experience before one is permitted to purchase and consume alcohol. By the age of 19, we are asked to contribute to society, through democracy and voting as well as the draft and military service. If one can demonstrate responsibility by this age, one should be given broader opportunity to show respect for society.

Fortunately, current laws provide us with a unique opportunity for a trial basis. A handful of states could lower the drinking age for a temporary period of 3 years, while studies are performed to gauge the full impact. By enacting these changes on a state level, we run trials in the regions of the county where the local population are willing participants.

Needless to say, underage drinking occurs in this country. In some cases it is encouraged by society through the glorification of wild parties and the allure of spring break. Does it make sense to expend resources in an attempt to forbid something we openly encourage through public media? It is not until one is in their presumed junior year of college that they turn 21, yet it is naive to think drinking does not occur at college until then. College drinking has become part of the fabric of American society, to some an act of growing up. If our goal is to prohibit this, then we are doing a poor job.

Ultimately, we as a country need to replace the current system of tying the minimum drinking age into federal highway funding. Each individual state should have the ability to set their legal drinking age without any repercussion from the federal government.

In the end if we act responsibly, and adhere to the requirements previously presented, we can adjust our laws to better fit with American culture. When laws follow common sense society is more willing to abide and respect the democratic system as a whole. When our laws fail to align with the values of society, confusion and disagreement persists. It should therefor be the consideration of elected officials to reduce the legal drinking age to match American culture.

# NOTES

*Does your first drink hold any special meaning?*

# Life,
# Aborted

*The emphasis must be not on the right to abortion but on the right to privacy and reproductive control.*

-Ruth Bader Ginsburg

*Erica was busy the summer she turned 19: recently accepted to a top regional university, she was busy preparing and saying goodbye to her high school friends. She was also uneasy about what do with her boyfriend of 3 years. Although they loved each other, he just entered the military and was about to be sent overseas. Then in late June she missed her period. With a promising future ahead of her and so much committed, a big decision weighed on her mind and she headed for the Assisted Life Clinic. And while the cost of the procedure didn't deter her; and neither did the ultrasound of the fetus; in the end the choice to sacrifice a life for the sake of her own was too much to bear. So for the second time in her life, Erica walked out of the procedure room with life altering consequences. Now, as she journeyed on her next quest, she understood where she would get help and how she just might pull it off.*

The decision to terminate an early stage pregnancy is a topic most people stray away from; the morality of the decision arising only when the situation is presented in front of you. Until then, to do the right thing is wishful thinking. But the right thing is not always so black and white: a pregnancy resulting from rape, a diseased or malformed fetus, or a mother's life put into danger by carrying to term.

In some cases however, abortions are used as a form of birth control, a way to prevent a mistake. Abortions also call into question the civility of society. If killing a pregnant woman can be treated as double homicide, why aren't abortions criminal? Combined with religious values, and it is easy to see how complicated this personal topic can be.

Yet a law can only go so far when it comes to intimate decisions. Defunding clinics do not prevent abortions from happening, but merely make them harder to perform. Whether law and society agrees with the moral decision, early term pregnancies have been terminated throughout history. Therefore it is imperative that we provide as safe as an environment as possible, not just for the potential mother, but for the unborn child as well. This will require properly funding and regulating clinics, as well as a functioning national adoption agency so that newborns can be taken care of and properly placed.

Ultimately a decision is made when one finds out they are pregnant and traditionally this is viewed as a woman's choice. This unborn child, however, is not created by, nor the sole offspring of a woman. While she may be the child bearer, it requires one other person to create the fetus, and society as a whole to raise and care for that child. A decision of such magnitude cannot be taken lightly and needs to involve more than one person. Whether society is pro-life or pro-choice or both, we have injected ourselves into each other's upbringing.

An abortion procedure is not a no-strings attached choice; quite contrary, there are personal consequences for a decision this deep. When a woman walks into a clinic, one way or another, the decision lives on for the rest of her life. To suggest otherwise is to degrade the morals of humanity.

Above all, the purpose of humanity is to survive from one generation to the next, by definition a pro-life stance. But we must also respect the parent's right to choose; as sexually active adults, we bear this responsibility. That choice however does not come without consequences, to both our maker and to society. As we facilitate this discussion, we must decide what, if any, that societal consequence should be.

Well, from a moral prospective, is it possible to define life? Where does the line between a fetus and unborn child exist? It has been suggested that life begins at the earliest stage in a pregnancy that science is able to resuscitate and sustain the fetus. In other words, at what point during the development of life, can we independently bring the child's life to term?

To date, the earliest a child has survived a premature pregnancy is at 25 weeks. However to remove ambiguity, and account for realistic fluctuation in science, the cutoff date should always be weeks prior. At that point it is inhuman to terminate life that which we as society could sustain and nurture. Therefore **an abortion is defined as the termination of a conceived life before it reaches sustainability**. Until a fetus can survive (with or without medical assistance) outside the child bearer's body, it is not considered an individual life. Understandably, many will disagree with this interpretation, but for the sake of simplicity, it is the most prudent definition.

As stated before, however, the availability of an

abortion should not be used as a form of birth control; there must be repercussions for the abuse of the procedure. While parents to-be should have the right to choose, society must also reinforce responsible decisions. For example, society can enforce restrictions for irresponsible behavior such as persistent early termination procedures.

In other situations, judgment must be reserved. Rape and a resulting pregnancy is a failure of society, and we must do more to prevent such horrid atrocities. It is also unmoral to force a child-bearer to sacrifice her own life for the sake of a full term pregnancy. We must approach these situations with a kind and gentle ear; no one asks to be put in this position.

Ultimately, the decision to have an abortion is a deeply personal one. The choice weighs heavily, not just on the child bearer, but also on the partner, and society as a whole. In order to survive, humanity must be pro-life, both for the life of the woman, and the life of the unborn child. In either case, we should not put restrictions on the decision to choose. By no means is an easy topic to discuss, but it is something that must take place. However we cannot regress as a country concerning a personal right to choose and imposing free will.

## *NOTES*

*Look at yourself and start to live again...*

# Strength and Honor

*I must study politics and war, that my sons may have the liberty to study mathematics and philosophy…in order to give their children the right to study painting, poetry, and music.*

-President John Adams

On May 2nd, 2011, two apache helicopters flew into Pakistani airspace unbeknownst to the rest of the world. On board, twelve of our nation's most elite soldiers, carrying along a mission of justice. After a decade of covert missions and intense searching, these twelve men snuck into a military compound with instructions to capture or kill Osama Bin Laden. For America, justice has no limits. Our country moved heaven and earth to locate this individual and with elite specialized force, was able to bring swift justice. On September 11th, when injustice fell upon us, we united as one and stood up to terror. On May $2^{nd}$ our military proved there is no place for evil in this world.

In the $21^{st}$ century, having the strongest military is more than having nuclear capabilities or organizing the largest army. The world's strongest military needs to be agile and adapt to the ever-changing environment around us: the natural environment, the complexities that dictate the world economy and the geo-political situations that are perpetually evolving.

Today, the strongest military acts as a deterrent against the forces of evil. The strongest military has a presence in the land, sea, air, space, and cyber, capable of attacking with swift and pinpoint accuracy. It will invokes fear in the adversary, forcing the enemy to think twice before attacking. It is also well trained and constantly improving to cover all weaknesses.

The strongest military is found in the United

States of America.

More than just a physical force, our military is a cohesive unit, able to secure our national safety. Our Special Ops strikes fear and confuses the enemy. Our Army ensures peace by preventing war. Our Navy deploys the utmost coordination and strong internal communication. Our Air Force provides many avenues to attack, yet is able to coordinate and efficiently respond to threats.

The presence of a strong military however, leads to more than just national safety and prosperity. It is a force to deter villains of humanity and prevent evil from spreading. A strong military is much more than deterrence, as it is used to enforce the civility of humanity across the globe.

Yet our military comes at a cost, not just financially, but of lives and resources as well. Many are ultimately sacrificed in order to preserve the ideals of human liberty; *only the good die young*. Maintaining the strongest military presence requires a devoted nation; not by a few, but as a united cohesive unit. When World War II broke out, our country banded together, sacrificing capitalism for the sake of humanity. This ultimately led not only to the perseverance of the human race, but also to the expansion of one of the most prosperous economies in recent history.

The science and technology required to drive our military forward has been responsible for major economic breakthroughs: the Internet was born out of a

DARPA project in order to facilitate faster communication between military research centers; GPS was developed by the military in order to better locate and pinpoint war machines. *The list goes on.*

Perhaps these technologies may have been developed regardless of our military incentive. But by striving to have the most advanced and respected military force, we have in turn developed technologies that drive the world economies. The breakthroughs our country has developed in order to maintain our position as a global military leader have been astonishing.

The United States leads with the strength of force, using it as a deterrent to eradicate evil from the globe. Developing and maintaining the strongest military has given us technological purpose to move forward. In turn, this has enabled us to protect human rights and enforce the American ideal of free liberty across the globe.

However, to reach the true pinnacle of global power, a country must not only be a deterrent of evil, and a leader of global innovation and technology, it must also be willing to cede decision of power. The U.S. should not only strive to be protect human rights, we must also cooperate with other nations to achieve this. Adhering to a global organization such as the U.N. facilitates a consensus of justified force. To go alone in this world, would surely lead to our downfall, no matter how advanced or innovative we might become.

It should follow that this is America and the

Globe, not America's Globe. The true distinction lies in our country's willingness to cooperate and use force only when necessary.

A strong military therefore possesses more than a nuclear bomb and pinpoint lethality. It requires pushing the envelope of human ingenuity and developing cutting edge technology. In the end a strong military listens to the human lives it protects and prospers into the future with minimal casualties. For as strong as a military may be, it is only as weak as the destruction it causes on the way to get there. War is evil; the United States has a responsibility to do everything it can to prevent it. We only survive war; we do not win.

# NOTES

*Is war the only path to peace?*

# Tragedy Of Life

*As one whose husband and mother-in-law have died the victims of murder and assassination, I stand firmly and unequivocally opposed to the death penalty for those convicted of capital offenses... An evil deed is not redeemed by an evil deed of retaliation.*

-Coretta Scott King

When the United States executed Troy Davis in 2011, they thought they had the right man. After all, they had spent millions of dollars and over two decades in the court system. Then the unthinkable happened: new evidence threw his guilt into question. Now the system was awash, did they execute an innocent man? Unfortunately, this case is not isolated. Many sitting on death row have proclaimed their innocence, and if only one acquitted person is executed, then the entire legal system and the penalty of death is called into question.

In our country, the death penalty is a contentious issue: In the 1970s it was outlawed by a Supreme Court ruling, only to be enabled again after a separate ruling. Our legal system and overall justice in the United States depends on crime and punishment; commit a crime against a person or society, and you will be punished. A court system with independent judges and a jury of peers is used to determine guilt. Depending on the severity of the crime, one can expect consequences ranging from community service to a life sentence. The ultimate punishment, reserved for the most horrific crimes, is the death penalty. In effect, this is used as a deterrent, but is it really?

Capital punishment is also utilized to help provide closure. But in some cases it does the exact opposite: families continue to suffer and the thought of taking another life becomes a moral burden.

Many times with an extended trial the reasonable expectation of fair and swift justice is lost. Those on death row often wait for up to 10 years, while local and federal governments spent millions of dollars to ensure the verdict. This is injustice to the victim and society.

Unfortunately after decades of implementation, the death penalty has provided neither a deterrent against horrific crimes nor a sense of justice and closure for society and those immediately affected. It is time to change this barbaric action.

The criminal and justice system is by no means perfect; however there must be a system in place to deter violent crimes. Justice as well as closure must be provided without burdening the victim's family. Finally we must accomplish this without years in the court system and the expenditure of millions of dollars.

As we reviewed the criminal system earlier, it was noted that locking away guilty individuals represents a lost opportunity and a burden to society that is unreasonable. The death penalty is another example of this injustice. As society, we need to be fair and reasonable with our punishment system, and expect criminal debt be paid back in full.

In an effort to provide justice, those who commit horrific crimes must be required to contribute back to society the life(s) taken. Through a series of choices, the criminals took it upon themselves to decide to end someone's life, and now they must live with their decision and actions, as we are forced to. In a simplified example, if a murderer takes a teacher's life, it should be demanded that the criminal's existence be dedicated to improving the education system. Admittedly, this is easier said than done, but execution is short-sited and serves little purpose.

Alternatively, if a criminal requests the death penalty, society should embrace that choice. From organ donors, to clinical research, their minds and bodies can serve society in far better ways than a lethal injection. If we are able to push the envelope of medicine, using those who are guilty of committing horrific crimes, then why shouldn't we? This is an opportunity for a criminal to make whole on the life they stole from society.

True closure must involve the victim's family and those personally affected. Some may choose to forgive, while others will want revenge. If possible, the victim's family will be involved in determining the debt the guilty must pay back to society. This may be easier said than done, but it is far better off then ending another one's life.

Ultimately, we must also take into account the cost of performing executions and the burden they place on the court system. Society, as well as the victim's family, deserves the right to a speedy trial and reasonable justice as well. One tragedy is enough, dragging out the trial only deepens the wound.

We can no longer, in the 21st century, continue a pattern of an eye for an eye; we must require criminals and those guilty of horrific crimes to give back to society. This may not act as a great deterrent, but in most cases, there is no deterrent great enough to prevent these crimes. We must therefore expect the guilty to make whole on their decision when they robbed our society of a life.

Crime, punishment, and the pursuit of justice; the death penalty is supposed to provide this and more. Clearly, murdering an individual for the sake of closure does not achieve this and therefore the death penalty should be should be abandoned.

# *NOTES*

---

*Death is the ultimate penalty…*

# ADULT

# E.D.U.

*I was bold in the pursuit of knowledge, never fearing to follow truth and reason to whatever results they led.*

-President Thomas Jefferson

*E rica, now at the young age of 32, was already familiar with the Adult EDU program: in the beginning, AEDU had helped her with parenting tips and basic financial management; but as her daughter grew, so did her needs. Erica now needed a higher paying job, one that required training so that she could better support her family. Once reluctant of SEDU and AEDU, Erica now embraced the programs to improve the well being of her family and herself.*

The United States, since its inception in 1776, has embraced many social programs in order to better its citizens. From public education for the young, to Medicare for seniors, we as a society have committed to taking care of ourselves. But programs that help us throughout our life, particularly in the middle of our career, seem to be non-existent. Our society should be working to improve a citizen's life each step of the way.

There should be no question that the citizens of America deserve the opportunity for continual education. Some of us are late bloomers; figuring out what we want to do only after public education has ended. Today, going back to school requires taking on large sums of debt, making the idea of continued education financially impossible. Others find themselves left behind by the ever-changing world economy. When jobs get shipped off to foreign nations, our citizens become stuck looking for non-existent jobs.

Education and training is a civil right every American deserves, not just to better themselves, but to help maintain the quality of life our country has created.

Therefore, an Adult Education program needs to be embraced if we are to maintain our position as a dominant leader in the global economy. In order to develop and ensure this program is efficiently tied into the private sector, several requirements exist:

First and foremost, this program needs to be fully funded, self sufficient, and operating on a balanced budget. This is not a profitable program, nor is it a charity. In order to facilitate funding and drive support to the private sector, the federal government should re-allocated taxable corporate funds to help sustain these programs.

Secondly, there needs to be financial incentives for citizens to participate. While many people who participate in the AEDU program will go on to earn higher wages, there also needs to be a short-term gain. For example, we can provide tax reductions for those that complete AEDU programs, knowing that expenditures will be recuperated through increased economic growth.

But the benefits of the AEDU program extend far beyond an individual citizen. Providing a training and learning center for adults will enable an elastic workforce that bends with the economic hardships. No longer will the workforce be under-qualified for the job opportunities that the global private sector demands. When the global economy changes direction (as it did when we left the industrial age, and now as we enter the technical age) our country will be better prepared and have to tools to adjust our workforce that makes America great.

In effect, AEDU will enable our country to quickly bounce back and pick up those left behind during tough economic times. Those that no longer have the skills to meet the demands of the industry will be able to retrain and better purpose themselves for the future. For example, those that have been displaced by the manufacturing robotics industry can now be trained to repair, design, and build the robotics. This enables the unemployed to reintegrate back into society.

We can also utilize the AEDU programs as a path towards citizenship for legal residents. Those who are here legally, but are not yet full citizens of America deserve the opportunity to become a functioning and contributing members of society. We can lift up those seeking a better opportunity in our country with immigration education. Those that are dedicated to the American dream, will receive certification and be on their way to becoming U.S. citizens. They will also be prepared for the opportunities that await them in the private sector, i.e. jobs with taxable income.

Fortunately, there are many topics that can be taught in AEDU programs. We can provide retirement planning, parenting tips, job retraining, health and fitness guidelines, and many other adult best practices. To provide continued flexibility, each state should facilitate different themes and adjust their classes to meet the demands of the local job force.

As a specific example, the AEDU can be

implemented as a one year program starting and January and lasting into December. This way, year after year, we unite a group of Americans and residents whom are all bettering themselves; unity in a graduation class bringing us closer together. Only when we cooperate and work together are our dreams fulfilled. Additionally, we will provide flexible class hours and coordinate hands on training to help answer questions, monitor progress, and provide feedback. We should also provide free day care and babysitting so that parents are enabled to attend.

Ultimately, Americans want to fulfill our dream, live in prosperity, and leave a better place for our kids. As the world economy continues to be ever dynamic, it is imperative that we make sure we are prepared for the changes that lie ahead. If we are able to retrain, readjust, and pivot to growth, then we can ensure prosperity for the indefinite future.

Past generations of America expanded and grew to where the jobs and opportunity lay. This is in essence the American Dream: the land of opportunity. Unlike our ancestors however, the opportunity is not across an ocean but right here in front of us. We are that opportunity, waiting to be untapped. It is time we use the resources at hand and invest back into our future. A fully sustainable Adult Education program is key to materializing the new American Dream.

## NOTES

*Do we ever stop learning?*

# Middle Ground

*In the Middle East, the conflict today is a matter of generations and not of cultures.*

-Shimon Peres

$A$s we travel out of the United States, we discover a variety of countries with unique governing bodies. Some are democratic and give life and hope to the people, others are authoritarian and repress their citizens. Each country, and the people that make up that nation, operates with different purpose. Some are conquerors, looking to expand their control and influence on the surrounding region. Others seek peace and mind their own business.

However, only a few countries actually impact us on a daily basis: the U.S. and its control on the global economy; China and its influence on manufacturing; Europe as a test bed for integrating policy. But no region has a bigger impact than the Middle East.

The Middle East for centuries has been a source of conflict. Whether it is a fight for resources, or a fight to exist, the region has always been an area of contention. Peace in the Middle East seems as far fetched as walking on water. Yet, it must happen. Humanity will forever struggle as long as there is conflict in the Middle East.

Every clash in that region can be traced to the land of Israel and the Holy City of Jerusalem. The site of the second temple and the Western Wall is a religious mecca not only for Jews but Christians and Muslims as well. Through historical context, peace can be achieved.

Today, conflict stems from Israel, the Palestinians, and a proposed two-state solution. The idea of a two-state solution has been suggested for the better part of three decades, but to no avail could leaders agree to the terms. As recent as 2017, Israel has endorsed a policy of settling into the disputed land. The opposition responds by launching rockets and staging attacks. Israel then cuts off aid and vital supplies to the region, creating what the World Health Organization calls, 'the most deplorable region in the world.' The opposition then takes to the streets, leading chants of 'Death to Israel'. This downward spiral of mistrust and aggression can not be allowed to fester.

After the Holocaust, a saying emerged in Jewish culture: **Never Again.** Interpreted as *Never again will we allow ourselves to perish*, while others have insisted *Never again will we allow human extermination*. It is not so much Israel has a commitment to prevent another Jewish Genocide, but rather to prevent all Genocides. If we look at the region however and the current state of the Israel and Palestine conflict, clearly **Never Again** is closer than is should be.

For decades, the United States has been instrumental in trying to broker peace between the two sides. As a collection of citizens with moral and human interests, it should become a priority of the United States, and our allies, to secure peace in the region, no matter the cost. Without peace between Israel and the region, there will never be peace in the world.

The history of the land plays an important part to understand what our possibilities are moving forward. Unfortunately, it takes years to review, and even more time to understand. A turning point however was the recreation of Israel in 1948: land was allocated as a place of sanctuary for Jews seeking refuge. Once the veil of atrocities from World War II was removed, it was clear that millions perished as the Jewish people had nowhere to escape to during the conflict.

So a map was drawn, borders laid out, and the state of Israel was created. Unfortunately it hasn't been that simple as factoring groups have been vying to control this land long before humanity discovered war. It should come as no surprise then that borders on a map didn't change that. Religious literature in various cultures often describes this land as 'The Promised Land' but recently it seems more like it is 'The Promised War.'

Faith is funny though and if peace is possible, and we should never give up that dream. If an Israeli Arab can break bread with a Palestinian Jew, than surely their two governing nations can find common ground. Peace will not be delivered overnight however, as issues will take generations to overcome. But we can do better.

To the opposing groups, who both lay claim to the same land: if we cannot inhabit land in a peaceful manner, than we should not live on it at all. Let us turn disputed areas into parks or memorials; burial grounds for those who have died fighting for this land. The United States should commit to building a memorial, a Statue of Unity, as reminder that there is something much bigger and important than conflict.

Truthfully, both sides of conflict must accept

blame for the current state of affairs. A token of peace must be provided, not just by leaders, but by the people in order for a serious treaty to take place. Hamas and the controlling groups of Gaza and the West Bank must put an end to firing rockets over Israel. Conversely, Israel must provide aid and safety for those living in all afflicted areas. Opposition groups must recognize Israel's right to exist and Israel must also stop its coordinated effort of settling into disputed land. Adhering to these stipulations would be the biggest milestone towards peace since the creation of Israel.

But we cannot stop there: an end to hostility is the ultimate goal. Peace is possible because of commonality in humanity: we all eat, drink and breathe from the same resources. This earth requires sharing for life to prosper; otherwise we all perish. **We must learn to live in harmony.**

Ultimately, we discuss the Middle East not because we have an interest in the region or its resources, but because the land is so volatile and that source of conflict spills into many regions of the world. While striving for peace in one region, we will be securing it in other places as well.

It is in our best interest as humans to promote compromise and allow the Middle East to be a symbol hope for the rest of the world. It is time we change the destiny of that region.

# NOTES

*Is conflict not the promise of the land?*

# People's Initiative

*Nobody will ever deprive the American people of the right to vote except the American people themselves and the only way they could do this is by not voting.*

-President Franklin D. Roosevelt

Listen closely as we choose our words carefully. We Americans need to bond together and brace ourselves for the storm that is abreast. We are stronger as a nation when we unite and support each other. From the civil right's movement, to women's suffrage and sexual equality, it is time for us all to unite and finish what each group started. This isn't a conservative or liberal movement; this is a revolution for the Common People. A time comes to re-institute checks and balances with the federal government; that time is now.

The American public can no longer trust and empower those currently in office to work for the people. We must uphold our constitutional responsibility and vote. As citizens of this country, voting is our most peaceful and effective tool of dissent.

As a collective, the federal government has failed our nation. Over the past few decades our institutions have become strife with angst, corruption, and complete dysfunction. However we are not blameless victims; on the contrary, we set up this system and voted these officials into power. Nonetheless, the political system has been morphed to provide the illusion that common people have a say in what happens in this country.

As citizens, we pay taxes into a system that has failed to prepare for the threats that confront us in the 21st century. Our roads and bridges are crumbling and our education system is no longer a model for success. This is the fault of our elected officials that manage this country. As voters, it is time for the people of this country to take back control and prevent the collapse of the United States.

Through voting and legislation, citizens can enact policies that shift power back to the people. Too much is at stake and no longer can we sit idle and wait for officials to do their job. The demands are simple: accountability, cooperation, and effectiveness.

Or are we as dysfunctional as those we have elected? Nay, America can do better; we demand greatness. An initiative of this magnitude will require a two-pronged solution:

The first step will require impactful change; to unite together and institute a mechanism for citizens to bypass elected officials. Previously we asked officials to write laws that limit their own power; this fallacy has laid waste to corruption and abuse of power. To expect self-limiting control of elected officials is no longer sustainable.

Secondly, once a mechanism is in place for the voters to bypass Congress and the self-governing power, a periodic maintenance needs to take place in order to prevent this country from falling into this barren again. Fixing the governing establishment requires a long-term fix, not something that can be adjusted in one bill.

A solution to our dysfunctional government will require more than a newly elected President or a change in controlling political party; we are demanding radical change in how our elected officials represent the values of the American People.

The people's initiative proposes a constitutional amendment that creates a framework to give power back to the people. Every two years, on the first and third years of a President's term, a voter created bill will be on the ballot. Representatives and employees of the government will be bared from voting on this bill; an attempt to give direct governing power back to the people. The amendment will also place term limits on all elected officials to encourage turnover and prevent a hold on power. We also propose tying elected official's salaries to the minimum wage and abolishing the federal pension program and generous health care. Becoming an elected official is an honor: there is no need to pay benefits after the representation has expired.

Ultimately, this new mechanism will enable the voting population to propose bills, create new legislation, and vote united as a general public. The best ideas will be put forth on the voter initiative ballot, regardless of party affiliation, or origin of idea. We are creating a process in which voters can bypass and control the legislative branch of our federal government.

At some point during the formation of our country, the people and founding fathers rose up against the British monarch. The Boston Tea party was their catalyst for change, what will be ours? Perhaps it is the rise of violence and mass shoots; or maybe it is the runaway debt we now face; others will point to a disenfranchised voter, who longer no believes a vote counts; perhaps it is the crumbling infrastructure, the poor quality of health care, or the complete lack of respect those in power hold for us and one another. Whatever our catalyst, we must act promptly; the longer we delay the harder to gain back control.

In the end, we must discuss our ideas, be willing to compromise on the path forward, and take unified action to force change. Whether you agree with the ideas of your American neighbor or not, we must work together. It is better to have a functioning government you disagree with, rather than a dysfunctional group of individuals vying for control. Cooperation is paramount; we must step up.

*It is an idea that will forever flourish in this nation: the idea that we can do better. **This is the American Dream;** to improve and leave something better behind. Do not forget this, and do not allow the American Dream to die; it is the corner stone of all that is great. May God bless you; and may God bless The United States of America.*

# *NOTES*

*Let us discuss.*

sistemas que componen al ser vivo y por último al individuo en sí.

El agua se encuentra en abundancia en nuestro planeta, sin embargo, no toda es apta para consumo humano, veremos también que la hace adecuada para nuestro uso y que consideraciones debemos tener antes de consumir cualquier tipo o calidad del agua.

La contaminación del agua que nos rodea es también un tema muy importante que no debemos dejar pasar, pues nos incumbe directamente a todos.

El agua que bebemos nosotros mismos y la que le permitimos a nuestra familia que consuma debe tener unas características de calidad mínimas, y también unas condiciones ideales para que lo llevemos directamente al seno de nuestro hogar.

La tecnología también nos puede ayudar en esta difícil tarea de buscar las condiciones ideales para que nuestra familia pueda gozar de los verdaderos beneficios del agua de excelente calidad.

Estudios alrededor del mundo, con diversos investigadores, universidades, laboratorios y centros de estudios clínicos, convergen en resultados muy similares en cuanto a las condiciones y características ideales que debe tener el agua, la razón por la que el agua debe tener estas características y la manera en que se pueden conseguir, ya sea de manera natural o de manera artificial.

El agua también puede contener algunos elementos dañinos para el ser humano, y no siempre es sencillo eliminarlos, es pues primordial, saber de que manera pueden evitarse éstos elementos y el daño que pueden ocasionar a nuestra familia.

Algunos elementos que debe contener el agua, son también

considerados como nutrientes para el cuerpo, ya que activan ciertas funciones en diversos sistemas y organismos para que optimicen su funcionamiento y así provean las condiciones adecuadas para que el cuerpo entre en estado de salud, y no solo de manera temporal, sino de manera permanente.

Estar sano es el estado natural del cuerpo, las enfermedades y malestares son desviaciones provocadas por elementos del medio ambiente o derivado del consumo de toxinas, y una de las funciones del agua es precisamente el acarreo de estas sustancias hacia el exterior del cuerpo, devolviéndole su estado de salud.

# Capítulo 1

## *Importancia del Agua*

### El Agua, ácida o alcalina

Empecemos por el tema del PH.

El llamado PH es una medición de acidez-alcalinidad de una solución líquida, se representa mediante una tabla de valores que van desde el cero que indica una acidez extrema y altamente corrosiva hasta el 14, que se refiere a una BASE o un líquido completamente alcalino, considerando exactamente el 7 como PH neutro.

La forma de equilibrar el PH de una solución es añadir una segunda solución con PH contario a la primera en cantidades suficientes hasta lograr el resultado deseado.

En nuestro cuerpo tenemos distintos fluidos con PH adecuado a la función que desempeñan y los procesos que realiza, por ejemplo:

**Fluido**                     **Rango de PH**

o  Sangre                      7.35 a 7.45

o  Saliva                      6.5 a 7.0

o  Esófago                     6.8 a 7.5

- o   Orina                         4.5 a 8.0

(Dependiendo que se esté eliminando)

- o   Estómago                      1.5 a 4.0

(Función corrosiva para digestión)

- o   Intestinos                    7.2 a 8.5


En general nuestro cuerpo tiene PH alcalino, y es de suma importancia mantenerlo así para su correcto funcionamiento, lo que hace muy lógico pensar que nuestros alimentos y el agua que consumimos debe ser alcalina, y de hecho lo es… pero en su forma más pura en la naturaleza, tanto el agua como frutas y vegetales son alcalinos cuando los encontramos en su forma más natural.

Con los avances tecnológicos aplicados sin cuidado a la nutrición, hemos roto el equilibrio del PH de nuestro cuerpo, y lo hemos llevado a niveles ácidos en los que no puede vivir adecuadamente, las funciones vitales no se llevan a cabo correctamente y un envejecimiento prematuro de células y órganos ha sido evidente, así como la presencia de enfermedades atípicas.

Es importante saber que envejecemos prematuramente y nos enfermamos más allá de lo normal debido a un exceso de acumulación de ácido en nuestro cuerpo, y que la alcalinidad neutraliza ese ácido; de tal forma que tomar agua alcalina tiene sentido si lo que buscamos es un estado de nuestro cuerpo más saludable.

**Pero, ¿sabemos cómo el agua alcalina trabaja en nuestro cuerpo?**

Algunas personas creen que la acidez del estómago contrarresta la alcalinidad del agua, por lo tanto aseguran:

**"tomar agua alcalina es inútil".**

¿Cómo contestamos a eso? ¿Ha pensado en esto alguna vez?

Esto es lo que pasa en el estómago:

El estómago mantiene un pH alrededor de 4.0. Cuando tomamos agua alcalina con un pH alto, el pH del agua baja y como resultado el pH del estómago sube buscando un equilibrio químico.

### ¿Qué tanto sube?

Esto es de acuerdo a la cantidad y al pH del agua alcalina que tome. Cuando el pH del estómago se eleva por encima de 4.5, el estómago producirá más ácido clorhídrico y lo pondrá en el estómago para colocar el pH del estómago por debajo de 4.0.

**¿Cómo es que el estómago produce ácido clorhídrico?**

Esto es algo que no ha sido descifrado ni por doctores, investigadores en medicina ni por los patólogos o algún otro científico aún.

*La fórmula química de la producción de ácido clorhídrico es:*

*$H_2O + CO_2 + NaCl = HCl + NaHCO_3$*

Agua, dióxido de carbono y cloruro de sodio (sal de mesa) produce ácido clorhídrico y bicarbonato de sodio. El ácido clorhídrico va al estómago, mientras que el bicarbonato de sodio va al torrente sanguíneo.

Un hecho interesante es que la fórmula arriba indicada se ve simple, pero NO hay científico en el laboratorio que haya podido hasta el momento, producir ácido clorhídrico y bicarbonato de sodio a partir del agua, dióxido de carbono y sal.

"SOLO CÉLULAS VIVIENTES PUEDEN HACER ESO".

En el laboratorio, revertir el proceso es fácil: adicionar ácido clorhídrico a bicarbonato de sodio producirá instantáneamente agua, dióxido de carbono y sal.

Los bicarbonatos entran al torrente sanguíneo sólo cuando el estómago produce ácido clorhídrico, por lo tanto el mayor aporte a la alcalinidad de nuestro cuerpo es cuando:

*TOMAMOS AGUA ALCALINA CON EL ESTÓMAGO VACÍO.*

La recomendación de la mayoría de los especialistas en nutrición, y médicos en general, es tomar 8 vasos de agua al día, es entonces el primero de ellos el que aporta una mayor cantidad de alcalinidad al torrente sanguíneo y, por lo tanto, es el mas importante de esos 8.

Ahora la reflexión será, ¿qué tipo de agua beberás en ese primer vaso del día?

Consideremos de nuevo la importancia de ese primer vaso, la alcalinidad es de suma importancia, y ese vaso podrá ser de café, refresco, agua azucarada, leche, etc. Sin embargo, ninguno de ellos fue un vaso de agua alcalina.

Los 8 vasos recomendados tienen que ser de agua sola o agua natural, sin sabores, azúcar, extracto de frutas, infusión de hierbas o cualquier otra cosa, tampoco cuenta el agua incluida en los alimentos como sopa o consomé.

La única manera de que el cuerpo administre ácido clorhídrico al estómago y por ende bicarbonato de sodio a la sangre es mediante alcalinizar el estómago vacío con por lo menos un vaso de 250 ml de agua alcalina.

El Bicarbonato de sodio es un regulador alcalino en la sangre.

En nuestra sangre hay reguladores alcalinos y reguladores ácidos que monitorean infatigablemente el pH de la sangre para mantenerlo constante en 7.365. Cuando la sangre se convierte en muy alcalina, el regulador ácido trabaja para bajar el pH y cuando la sangre se convierte en muy ácida, el regulador alcalino trabaja para elevar el pH.

Los reguladores alcalinos son bicarbonatos ($HCO_3^-$) aparejados con minerales alcalinos.

**Algunos ejemplos de éstos son:**

- Bicarbonato de sodio (**$NaHCO_3$**).

- Bicarbonato de potasio (KHCO3).

- Bicarbonato de calcio (Ca (HCO3)2)

- Bicarbonato de magnesio (**Mg ($HCO_3$)$_2$**).

**Los reguladores ácidos son mayormente:**

- Ácido carbónico (H2CO3).

- Combinación de agua y dióxido de carbono.

El hidrato de carbono quemado se convierte completamente en dióxido de carbono ($CO_2$) y agua ($H_2O$); de tal modo que no hay atajos para los reguladores ácidos.

# Descubrimiento de la Dra. Lynda Frassetto

En 1996, la **Dra. Lynda Frassetto**, de la

Universidad de California, San Francisco, descubrió y publicó* que a medida que envejecemos, empezando alrededor de los 45 años, perdemos reguladores alcalinos – **bicarbonatos** – en nuestra sangre. Para cuando cumplimos 90 años, hemos perdido el 18% de bicarbonatos en nuestra sangre.

*PUBLICACIÓN:

-Journal of Gerontology: BIOLOGICAL SCIENCE, 1996, Vol. 51A. No. 1, B91-B99. Por la Dra. Lynda Frassetto, de la Universidad de California, San Francisco, Ca.-

Una cantidad insuficiente de bicarbonatos en la sangre reduce nuestra capacidad de manejar (neutralizar y eliminar) el ácido que nuestro cuerpo produce. Esta es la principal causa del envejecimiento y muchas veces prematuro, por eso a los 45 años es la edad promedio cuando los seres humanos empiezan a mostrar síntomas de diabetes, hipertensión, osteoporosis y muchas otras enfermedades degenerativas. Y ya que no podemos manejar los ácidos, acumulamos desechos ácidos en el cuerpo; estos desechos se muestran como colesterol, ácido graso, ácido úrico, uratos, sulfatos, fosfatos, piedras en los riñones, etc.

## ¿Cuál es la propiedad más importante del agua alcalina?

El agua alcalina tiene muchas propiedades, como una adecuada tensión superficial para la absorción de ella en los tejidos, la estructura hexagonal de la molécula del agua, la medida molecular, reducción de oxígeno potencial, valor del pH, minerales alcalinos causantes de mantener el valor alcalino del pH, etc.

Aun cuando el valor del pH del agua es lo único que ayuda a la sangre a recibir bicarbonatos, todas las otras propiedades funcionan como una fuente de nutrición, aportando elementos para que el estómago produzca ácido clorhídrico que va a los jugos gástricos y bicarbonatos que van al torrente sanguíneo.

Sin embargo, la función más importante del agua alcalina es aumentar los bicarbonatos en la sangre porque perdemos bicarbonatos a medida que envejecemos.

Cuando decimos que alcalinizamos nuestro cuerpo, no necesariamente quiere decir que nuestro pH de la saliva o el pH de la orina subirán; pero significa que se elevaran los bicarbonatos en la sangre. El pH de la sangre no cambia, pero se eleva la habilidad de la sangre de neutralizar el ácido que entra o se generen en el cuerpo, resultado de estrés y otros factores en su mayoría externos.

En enero/febrero del 2003 una publicación del *"American Industrial Hygiene Association Journal,"* El **Dr. Gospodinka R. Pradova**, publicó los resultados de 10 años de estudio de la contaminación industrial en Bulgaria.

El estudio compara dos grupos de personas trabajando en una fábrica de plástico:

Un grupo trabaja en la planta expuesto a la contaminación química, el otro en un ambiente sin contaminación en las oficinas de la misma compañía. La conclusión muestra que las personas que viven o trabajan en un ambiente con contaminación tienen menos cantidad de bicarbonatos en la sangre que la gente que trabaja en un ambiente limpio.

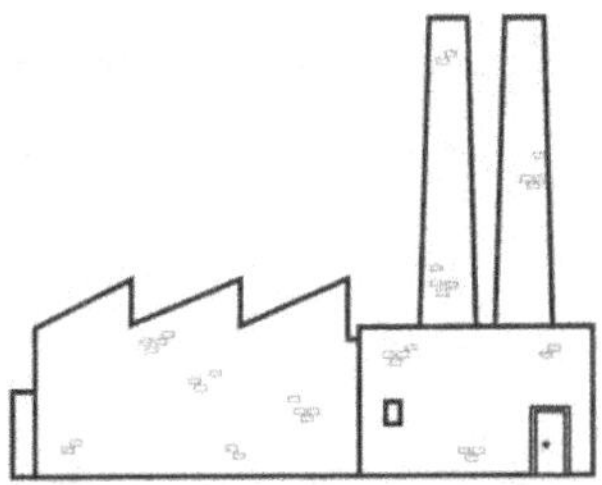

Vivimos en un mundo que ha cambiado de un ambiente agrícolacultural a un ambiente industrial, que produce más contaminación.

Nuestro estilo de vida estresado crea más ácido, que hace que usemos más bicarbonatos. Algunas comidas son más ácidas que otras, especialmente, carnes con altas proteínas y bebidas altamente ácidas. Estas son las razones de porqué perdemos bicarbonatos en la sangre a medida que envejecemos.

La sociedad médica considera la reducción de bicarbonatos en la sangre como un inevitable factor del envejecimiento.

*"Múltiples investigadores argumentan que la reducción de bicarbonatos en la sangre es la causa del envejecimiento y enfermedades y no el resultado de envejecer".*

Mientras reemplacemos bicarbonatos en la sangre, ¡no tenemos que envejecer de manera prematura!

## ¿CUÁNDO TOMAR AGUA ALCALINA?

Ya vimos que los bicarbonatos entran al torrente sanguíneo sólo cuando el estómago produce ácido clorhídrico, es importante que en ese momento tomemos agua alcalina con un valor pH lo más alto posible.

Es altamente recomendable tomar agua alcalina con el estómago vacío.

En un estómago vacío, el valor pH del estómago puede ser tan ácido como 1.5 de PH, pero el monto (volumen) de ácido clorhídrico en el estómago es pequeño; de esta manera, tomando 250 ml de agua con un pH mayor a 7 subirá el pH del estómago relativamente a un PH alto. Esto causará que el estómago produzca más ácido clorhídrico, y por lo tanto producirá y permitirá que más bicarbonatos entren al torrente sanguíneo.

Otro suceso, es que el agua alcalina puede entrar al intestino inmediatamente, ya que no hay comida sólida en el estómago para ser digerida. Cuando esto sucede, la sangre absorberá agua alcalina al torrente sanguíneo desde el intestino.

Dentro de los mecanismos automáticos del cuerpo, el regulador ácido (ácido carbónico $H_2CO_3$) interactuaría con el agua alcalina para disminuir el pH de la sangre y el regulador ácido se convertiría en un regulador alcalino.

$$Ca(OH)_2 + 2(H_2CO_3) = Ca+(HCO_3-)_2 + 2(H_2O)$$

Un incremento de bicarbonatos en el torrente sanguíneo previene el envejecimiento prematuro y ataca las enfermedades degenerativas.

Ahora conoces los mecanismos descifrados por los científicos de cómo el agua alcalina extiende la vida.

*Cuando pensamos en salud, pensamos en dieta y ejercicios. Pero ni dietas ni ejercicios adicionan bicarbonatos al torrente sanguíneo.*

El estudio ha sido basado en agua alcalina rica en hidróxido de calcio. Este tipo de agua es producido por un ionizador porque el mineral predominante en el agua de la mayoría de los suministros municipales es calcio.

Muchas variedades comerciales de agua reclaman tener beneficios de salud:

- Agua que da energía.

- Agua Pi.

- Agua de nieve derretida.

- Agua natural de manantial.

- Agua tratada magnéticamente.

- Agua con oxígeno.

- Agua estructurada hexagonal.

- Agua con partículas de Oro.

Y aunque lo importante es que el pH del agua sea alcalino (ya que sólo el agua alcalina con un pH alto adiciona bicarbonatos en la sangre), no podemos ignorar la calidad general del agua y los elementos que contienen como:

- Hongos

- Bacterias

- Virus

- Metales pesados

- Sales minerales

- Toxinas

- Químicos

Es entonces en donde **SI** importa también la calidad general del agua.

Algunas personas, normalmente sin bases científicas, sostienen que ingerir bicarbonatos (bicarbonato de soda o bicarbonato de sodio) sería como ingerir sal, porque nuestro estómago ácido lo descompondría en agua, dióxido de carbono y cloruro de sodio (sal) y ningún bicarbonato llegaría al torrente sanguíneo, pero ya vimos con detalle como es que esto funciona. Por otro lado, la sal no es un elemento que en grandes cantidades sea benéfico para el cuerpo humano, por lo que nadie especializado en salud, recomendará ingerir sal a cambio de bicarbonatos.

**¡SOLO EL AGUA ALCALINA PUEDE LLEVAR CARBONATOS AL TORRENTE SANGUÍNEO Y PROLONGAR SU VIDA!**

## AGUA Y PLATA COLOIDAL

## LA PLATA COLOIDAL DESDE TIEMPOS REMOTOS

*"La plata coloidal aniquila más de 650 especies de microbios patógenos en minutos".*

Desde principios del pasado siglo XX se sabe que ninguna bacteria, virus, Hongo, Levadura o microbio puede vivir en un líquido en el que haya una sola partícula de plata coloidal. Dicho metal los aniquila al contacto en sólo minutos. De ahí que la plata coloidal obtenida por electrolisis de plata pura se considere una de los más potentes y eficaces germicidas naturales conocidos y se le otorgue la denominación de ***súper-antibiótico***.

Sin efectos secundarios adversos a las dosis adecuadas, sin interaccionar con otros medicamentos y sin provocar reacciones de rechazo alérgicas, la Plata coloidal tiene una gran eficacia, además, por la rapidez con la que actúa y por su inocuidad se considera hoy a este antiguo remedio como una especie de segundo sistema inmune del que puede disponer el cuerpo humano.

 A pesar la capacidad de investigación y especialización de la industria farmacéutica, la experiencia demuestra que los microorganismos acaban desarrollando resistencia a todos sus sofisticados y carísimos antibióticos, lo que reduce o incluso anula su eficacia. Ante esta realidad, un número creciente de expertos aboga por la vuelta a un germicida considerado infalible, a un

clásico de la medicina natural cuyo uso se fue abandonando progresivamente a mediados del siglo pasado por el empuje de los antibióticos modernos, económicamente más lucrativos, pero de cuestionable eficacia en muchos casos.

Hablamos de la **PLATA COLOIDAL**, que tras décadas de olvido está siendo rescatada como remedio increíblemente eficaz en la prevención y tratamiento de enfermedades infecciosas. ¿Su aval? Su inigualable capacidad germicida:

*ELIMINA A MÁS DE 650 ESPECIES DE MICROORGANISMOS PATÓGENOS*

Demostrado en numerosos laboratorios de investigación alrededor del mundo.

Además, el hecho constatado de que, ante su presencia, cualquier microorganismo es eliminado de forma tan rápida que le es imposible generar mecanismos de resistencia. Se trata, en suma, de un remedio eficaz, natural, sin efectos secundarios a las dosis adecuadas y asequible que puede ayudarnos a prevenir numerosas enfermedades infecciosas y a recobrar y mantener la salud.

## Un remedio desde la antigüedad

El uso antibiótico de la plata data de civilizaciones tan antiguas como la griega y la romana, que también  utilizaban este metal para elaborar utensilios de cocina o recipientes dende almacenar y servir el agua.

Así lo recoge el historiador y geógrafo griego Heródoto (484-425 a.C.) considerado el padre de la historia, quien en sus escritos narra que, donde quiera que fuera el rey Ciro de Persia llevaba consigo una mula que transportaba recipientes de plata llenos de agua hervida y que sólo bebía de ellos.

Y es que según parece, ya entonces sabían que la **plata inhibe el crecimiento de microorganismos que estropean los alimentos, las bebidas y enferman al cuerpo de humanos y animales.**

Esa es, asimismo, la explicación de la costumbre de los primeros pobladores del Oeste americano que introducían un dólar de plata en los recipientes de leche para facilitar su conservación y evitar el crecimiento de hongos y bacterias. De hecho, en la actualidad se sigue confiando en la capacidad de la plata coloidal para eliminar una amplísima gama de organismos patógenos, lo que hace útil añadirla a los alimentos para aumentar el tiempo de su conservación, incluso para potabilizar el agua.

Esta propiedad la ha convertido en herramienta de utilidad extraterrestre ya que los rusos la utilizan para esterilizar el agua reciclada a bordo de las estaciones espaciales y la **NASA** eligió un sistema de tratamiento de aguas a base de plata coloidal para el puente aéreo espacial.

En cuanto a su uso terapéutico se tiene constancia de que tanto la Medicina Tradicional China como la Medicina Ayurvédica (medicina tradicional Hindú) han usado la plata **-sea sola, o combinada con otras sustancias-** como remedio para prevenir y tratar múltiples infecciones, como tónico rejuvenecedor para pacientes debilitados por alguna dolencia o simplemente por la edad.

Para esta última tradición médica, la plata es muy eficaz en el tratamiento de afecciones hepáticas y la usan también para *"refrescar mente, emociones y cuerpo en padecimientos tales como neuritis y neuralgia, inflamaciones de las membranas mucosas, enfermedades del sistema reproductor y mentales".*

Por lo que respecta a Occidente hasta le década de los 20´s del siglo pasado era común entre los médicos el uso de la plata coloidal para el tratamiento de decenas de enfermedades cuyo origen fueran virus, bacterias u hongos, así como para ayudar a cicatrizar heridas y quemaduras. Sin embargo, el aumento del precio de la plata y los costos de producción, así como el desarrollo de otro tipo de antibióticos más rentables llevarían a este germicida natural a un rincón olvidado del que hace aproximadamente cuarenta años intentan rescatarlo médicos y profesionales de la salud de todo el mundo. Gracias a ellos la plata coloidal empieza a ocupar de nuevo el lugar que nunca debió perder como antibiótico natural de referencia.

Ahora bien, el camino no es fácil pues su vuelta se enfrenta al todopoderoso *"establishment"* de la industria farmacéutica, nada interesado en que un producto tan económico, eficaz y fácil de usar esté al alcance de todos.

# CAPÍTULO 3

## *LA PLATA COMO NUTRIENTE*

### PARTÍCULAS EN SUSPENSIÓN.

Las investigaciones realizadas en las últimas décadas han revelado que mientras antiguamente el cuerpo humano obtenía una cantidad elemental -y necesaria- de

plata a través de la ingesta de frutas y

verduras frescas, en la actualidad la sobreexplotación de los suelos y la degradación de sus minerales - *en porcentajes que incluso superan el 80%* - ha hecho que carezcamos de este metal esencial. Pero ojo, porque no se trata de la mera carencia de un nutriente; los expertos señalan que la deficiencia de minerales como  plata y Zinc es uno de los factores que han hecho aumentar drásticamente los desórdenes del sistema inmune humano en los últimos años.

De ahí que se postule la necesidad de tomar la plata en su forma coloidal para suplir ese déficit y prevenir numerosas dolencias, especialmente las causadas por microorganismos patógenos.

Pero, ¿qué es la **plata coloidal**? Pues, en pocas palabras, plata y agua. Mas concretamente, minúsculas partículas de plata cargadas eléctricamente que se encuentran en suspensión *(recordamos en este punto al lector que los líquidos más importantes del cuerpo son coloidales, es decir, compuestos por partículas ultra finas en suspensión)* y se obtienen por electrólisis de plata pura 100% en agua destilada. De esta forma se desprenden partículas microscópicas de plata que se mantienen en suspensión gracias a la diminuta carga eléctrica de cada una de ellas.

Afirman los expertos que este minúsculo tamaño aumenta considerablemente la reactividad de la plata con los organismos unicelulares con los que entra en contacto de tal forma que éstos *-ya sean bacterias, hongos, virus, etc.-* se tragan las partículas de plata, algo que acaba propiciando su eliminación apenas en unos minutos.

También su tamaño extremadamente pequeño les permite penetrar más fácilmente en cualquier tejido y viajar a lo largo del cuerpo multiplicando su eficacia terapéutica.

Eso sí, quede claro que en todo momento hablamos del coloide de la plata (obtenido por un método fisicoquímico) y no del oligoelemento plata (que se obtiene específicamente por métodos químicos).

Hablando de oligoelementos, son los que por sobre dosificación, puede provocar argiria o manchas de color gris que tiñen de manera permanente la piel y las membranas mucosas, pero no para la plata coloidal, lo que hace importante, fijarnos de que fuente estamos obteniendo la plata para nuestra nutrición y la de nuestra familia.

En cuanto a la plata coloidal no se conocen efectos secundarios cuando ésta se prepara con la concentración adecuada, tampoco se han descrito casos de interacción con otras sustancias, no produce adicción ni intolerancia y los estudios demuestran que no se deposita bajo la piel sino que pasa a través del tracto digestivo hasta eliminarse por completo a través de las heces.

## UN AUTÉNTICO SÚPER ANTIBIÓTICO.

Investigaciones recientes llevadas a cabo en universidades y centros de investigación de todo el mundo han podido confirmar los hallazgos de nuestros ancestros e, incluso, ampliar el listado de sus bondades e indicaciones. Y así hoy se considera que la plata coloidal es un:

***"Potente germicida de amplio espectro"***.

 Ya en 1914 la revista *"The Lancet"* publicó los resultados de un estudio llevado a cabo por el **Dr. Henry Crookes** con plata coloidal que demostró que es altamente germicida e inofensiva para el cuerpo humano. En aquel artículo el investigador norteamericano afirmaba:

*"No conozco ningún microbio que no haya podido ser eliminado en el laboratorio con plata coloidal en un lapso máximo de 6 minutos, sin efectos secundarios negativos*

Recientes investigaciones realizadas en la Universidad de Carolina de los Ángeles (**UCLA, USA**) confirman que bastan solo 6 minutos *–muchas veces menos tiempo-* desde el contacto con la plata coloidal para que el germen muera.


Lo que hace la plata coloidal es inactivar las enzimas que las bacterias, hongos, virus, levaduras y otros microorganismos usan para su metabolismo del oxígeno, es decir, consigue inutilizar el pulmón químico de dichos parásitos y de sus formas plemórficas o mutantes y eliminarlas incluso en su etapa de huevos.

Por ese motivo, al contrario de lo que ocurre con los antibióticos sintéticos, el microorganismo no puede desarrollar mecanismos de resistencia ni ningún tipo de mutación que le permita escapar de la acción germicida de la plata.

Luego las células del sistema retículo-endotelial (**PARTE DEL SISTEMA INMUNE**) logran expulsar del cuerpo los gérmenes ya muertos. Por tanto, la plata coloidal funciona como un catalizador ya que su sola presencia hace que muchos microorganismos causantes de enfermedades infecciosas no puedan respirar y mueran asfixiados.

La plata coloidal ha demostrado hacer esto exactamente con 650 tipos diferentes de gérmenes.

En 1988 el doctor **Larry C. Ford** - Investigador de la escuela de medicina de la ya citada universidad de Californiana- demostró que los *streptococcus pyogenes, staphylococcus aureus, neisseria gonorrea, garnerella vaginalis, salmonella typhi* y otros microbios patógenos entéricos, así como la *candida albicans, la candida globata y la malassezia* entre muchos otros, son eliminados por completo en unos cuantos minutos. De ahí que el **Dr. Harry Margraf** (*bioquímico e investigador de la universidad de Saint Louis (USA), colaborador de la universidad de Washington y pionero en la investigación de la plata*) llegara a afirmar:

***"La plata coloidal es, sin duda, el mejor y más versátil combatiente de gérmenes que tenemos".***

Además, al contrario que los antibióticos sintéticos (que destruyen también las enzimas y las bacterias benéficas), la plata coloidal no provoca daño alguno ni a las enzimas ni a ningún otro componente del organismo humano, y es así porque sólo ataca a las enzimas de formas de vida unicelulares que son radicalmente diferentes a los organismos pluricelulares.

No debemos olvidar que dentro del cuerpo humano la plata coloidal no forma compuestos tóxicos ni reacciona con otra cosa que no sea la enzima metabolizadora de oxígeno de un germen unicelular. Por tanto, no puede causar rechazos o alergias de ningún tipo.

## PLATA COMO UN SEGUNDO SISTEMA DE DEFENSAS.

"La plata coloidal no sólo elimina los virus, bacterias y demás gérmenes capaces de generar enfermedades, sino que además fortalece nuestro sistema inmune y nos ayuda a prevenir numerosas dolencias, especialmente las de tipo infeccioso".

Así lo afirmaba ya a finales de la década de los 70 del siglo pasado el **Dr. Robert O. Becker** - cirujano ortopédico investigador en Medicina durante más de 30 años y considerado uno de los padres de la Electromedicina y la Electroquímica así como uno de los pioneros en el resurgir de la plata en aplicaciones médicas- que constató una correlación entre los valores bajos de plata en el cuerpo y los estados de enfermedad, fue el primero en afirmar que:

**"la deficiencia de plata es responsable del funcionamiento incorrecto del sistema inmune".**

En 1978 el Dr. Becker publicaría un estudio en el que se podía leer: *"Gracias a la investigación de mente abierta la plata coloidal está emergiendo como una maravilla de la medicina moderna. Un antibiótico pueda matar a quizás una docena de organismos patógenos diversos, pero la plata mata alrededor de 650 y sin que se generen mutaciones resistentes. Es más, además de acabar con los microorganismos causantes de enfermedades, la plata coloidal estimula de forma notable el sistema de defensas del cuerpo Humano".*

Y es que, como han corroborado investigaciones posteriores, tomada diariamente la plata coloidal proporciona, por su gran efectividad y por la rapidez y con la que actúa, un verdadero *"segundo sistema de defensas"* que produce energía vitalidad y vigor, reduce las toxinas del cuerpo (al aumentar el fluido y drenaje linfático lo que mejora la oxigenación, la regeneración de tejidos y el flujo de energía en el cuerpo), provoca una significativa elevación de glóbulos blancos en la sangre y genera una rápida sensación de alivio.


Se ha constatado que no afecta a las bacterias benéficas del intestino grueso porque la plata coloidal en dosis normales se absorbe en los primeros metros del intestino delgado. Y como no interactúa con ninguna sustancia del cuerpo no puede causar alergia o rechazo.

Según investigaciones de **Bringham Young University** (Utah, USA) la plata coloidal elimina el VIH, presunto virus causante del sida. Y aunque la FDA norteamericana no permite el uso del coloide de plata para tratar esta enfermedad ha autorizado ya su uso en las derivadas de un VIH activo.

## AYUDA A ELIMINAR LAS CÉLULAS TUMORALES.

El **Dr. Björn Nordström** - del Karolinska Institutet de Estocolmo (Suecia)- viene utilizando desde hace décadas la plata coloidal para el tratamiento del cáncer con resultados sorprendentes. De hecho, ha publicado varios casos de rápida remisión en pacientes desahuciados.

El **Dr. Gary Smith**, pionero en la investigación del cáncer, *Co-leader of the prostate Program for the Roswell Park Cancer Center Support,* afirma tras años de estudio, que de manera general el éxito de un tratamiento anticancerosos depende de la cantidad de plata coloide presente en el organismo, y que su fracaso es la consecuencia de la carencia de esa plata, de esta manera, enuncia en algunas de sus tantas publicaciones:

"CUANDO LA PLATA ESTÁ PRESENTE, LAS CÉLULAS CANCEROSAS SON DIFERENCIADAS Y EL CUERPO REESTABLECIDO. DE AHÍ QUE POSIBLEMENTE UNA DEFICIENCIA DE PLATA SEA UNA DE LAS MUCHAS

RAZONES DE QUE EXISTA EL CÁNCER Y DE QUE AUMENTE TAN RÁPIDAMENTE".

## REGENERACIÓN DE TEJIDOS

Promueve la curación de heridas y quemaduras, de hecho, se usa en las unidades de quemados de los principales hospitales por ser considerado como un potente antiséptico y un efectivo reparador de los tejidos. Y es que se ha comprobado que evita la infección, acelera el proceso de cicatrización y atenúa las cicatrices o marcas posteriores a las heridas o quemaduras.

## ESTIMULA EL CRECIMIENTO DE LOS HUESOS.

A finales de los 70`s del siglo pasado, el ya mencionado **Dr. Robert O. Becker** descubrió mientras estudiaba la capacidad de regeneración de los tejidos humanos, que la plata coloidal promueve el crecimiento del hueso. Observó que además eliminaba las infecciones circundantes sin dañar los tejidos sanos y reducía en promedio un 50% el tiempo de convalecencia en casos de fracturas.

**UNA AYUDA DURANTE EL EMBARAZO Y PARA EL FETO.**

Se ha comprobado que la plata coloidal favorece el crecimiento y la salud del feto, hace que el parto y la recuperación de la madre sean fáciles y rápidos.

A todo lo dicho hay que añadir que ayuda a aliviar la inflamación, mejora la digestión y es un reconstituyente general del organismo. De hecho, muchas personas que la toman a diario afirman sentirse más jóvenes y además se ven más jóvenes, y lo comprueban con la prueba de edad metabólica que por lo regular arroja una edad inferior a la real de la persona de hasta 15 años.

La explicación esta según los expertos, en que el cuerpo, gracias a las propiedades preventivas e inmuno potenciadoras de la plata coloidal, puede utilizar sus energías para otras tareas distintas a luchar constantemente contra las enfermedades.

En suma, la plata coloidal es una alternativa totalmente segura, barata, eficaz y sin efectos secundarios; además es efectiva contra las cepas microbianas que son resistentes a los antibióticos convencionales.

La plata coloidal según diversos estudios llevados a cabo principalmente durante el siglo pasado, es útil en el tratamiento de más de **650 afecciones diferentes** entre las que cuentan:

- Acné
- Alergias
- Amigdalitis
- Apendicitis
- Artritis
- Bursitis
- Cáncer
- Candidiasis
- Cistitis
- Cólera
- Colitis
- Infecciones de ojos, oídos, boca y garganta
- Congestión nasal
- Conjuntivitis
- Dermatitis
- Diabetes causada por una infección
- Diarrea
- Disentería
- Eczemas
- Envenenamiento de la sangre
- Erupciones

- ❖ Escarlatina

- ❖ Fatiga crónica

- ❖ Fibrosis

- ❖ Fiebre en general

- ❖ Forúnculos

- ❖ Gastritis (incluso las causadas por Helicobacter Pylori)

- ❖ Gingivitis

- ❖ Gonorrea

- ❖ Gripe estomacal

- ❖ Heridas abiertas

- ❖ Herpes zoster

- ❖ Indigestión

- ❖ Inflamación de la vejiga

- ❖ Irritación de la garganta

- ❖ Lepra

- ❖ Leucemia

- ❖ Lupus

- ❖ Malaria

- ❖ Melanoma

- ❖ Meningitis

- ❖ Mononucleosis

- ❖ Neumonía

- ❖ Neurastenia

- ❖ Oftalmia purulenta

- ❖ Parásitos en la sangre

- ❖ Pie de atleta

- ❖ Piorrea

- ❖ Pleuritis

- ❖ Problemas de tiroides

- ❖ Prurito anal

- ❖ Psoriasis

- ❖ Pulmonía (viral, fúngica o bacteriana)

- ❖ Quemaduras

- ❖ Queratitis

- ❖ Resfriado común
- ❖ Reumatismo
- ❖ Rinitis
- ❖ Seborrea
- ❖ Septicemia
- ❖ Sida
- ❖ Sífilis
- ❖ Sinusitis
- ❖ Tiña
- ❖ Tos
- ❖ Toxemia
- ❖ Tuberculosis
- ❖ Úlceras de estómago
- ❖ Verrugas.

# CAPÍTULO 4

## *ZINC EN EL AGUA*

### UN DIAMANTE DE LA NUTRICIÓN

El zinc ha sido estudiado relativamente hace poco, y la ciencia ha encontrado que es necesario para la realización de mas de 200 funciones en el interior de nuestro cuerpo, está directamente relacionado con el buen funcionamiento de numerosos órganos y sistemas, y niveles deficientes de Zinc han sido también relacionados con una gran cantidad de enfermedades.

El zinc tiene también la peculiaridad que el cuerpo no lo puede almacenar, por lo que los requerimientos diarios de Zinc deben ser consumidos al día, mantener entonces los niveles adecuados de Zinc será resultado definitivamente de mantener una dieta que incluya este mineral en cantidades suficientes para mantener el cuerpo sano.

Recientes estudios han descubierto que el Zinc es un importante ingrediente de las células inmunológicas, ya que los niveles apropiados de este elemento, estimula el desarrollo y funcionalidad de estas células, a lo que una deficiencia de este elemento propiciará fácilmente el inicio de procesos infecciosos en diversos órganos por permitir la entrada a agentes patógenos.

Se ha relacionado clínicamente que el descenso en la capacidad inmunológica tradicionalmente asociada a la edad, se ve revertida al incrementar los niveles de Zinc en la dieta de los pacientes, ayudando de manera importante a combatir numerosas enfermedades.

Este elemento también se sabe que es esencial para la correcta absorción de nutrientes provenientes de los alimentos, a tal grado que en hospitales por todo el mundo, administran una rica dieta en Zinc al tratar a personas con altos grados de desnutrición ya que ayuda de manera importante a que el cuerpo asimile los nutrientes que le son proporcionados por medio de los alimentos, por lo tanto, interviene directamente en la salud celular, al ayudar a su correcta nutrición.

En definitiva, una correcta nutrición celular trae como resultado inmediato, órganos más sanos, regeneración celular acelerado, correcto crecimiento y desarrollo de niños y adolescentes.

En la presencia de adecuados niveles de Zinc, el cuerpo tiene una recuperación más rápida frente a enfermedades ya sean de origen viral, bacterial o incluso celular como el cáncer.

Múltiples estudios se han enfocado directamente en el comportamiento de las células cancerosas en presencia del zinc, y hay una franca mejoría, ya que con una dieta rica en Zinc, los pacientes han superado la enfermedad.

Los tipos de cáncer que se han estudiado con magníficos resultados son cáncer oral, cáncer de esófago y estómago, cáncer de cabeza, cuello, pulmón vesícula biliar, próstata y cáncer de ovarios.

El zinc está relacionado también con los procesos digestivos, ya que estabiliza la mucosa intestinal, ayuda a la restitución de las células lesionadas en el sistema digestivo, acelera el proceso de reparación y regeneración de tejidos, ayuda a suprimir los procesos inflamatorios de estómago e intestinos ocasionados por las reacciones con algunos alimentos.

Otro proceso importante en el que el Zinc participa, es la nutrición cerebral, ya que el cerebro prácticamente funciona solo con Oxígeno, azúcar, agua y Zinc.

Numerosos estudios han comprobado que un bajo nivel de Zinc en la sangre, afecta directamente a procesos cognitivos desde memoria, concentración y aprendizaje que estaban relacionados al envejecimiento, pero ahora se ha podido demostrar que están más ligados al nivel de Zinc que a la edad , ya que al regular los niveles de este elemento en sangre, los procesos degenerativos cognitivos se revierten en una importante tasa, incluso aquellos que se consideraban incurables.

Niveles adecuados de Zinc y plata en la sangre, son la receta ideal para que a temprana edad, el desarrollo neuropsicológico, habilidades de atención y concentración, y como consecuencia el desempeño de los procesos mentales, habilidades motoras y de razonamiento se dé a su máxima capacidad, siendo entonces un importante elemento en el mejor desarrollo de los niños.

Los niños y jóvenes son quienes mas frecuentemente presentan niveles bajos de Zinc en sangre, ya que su requerimiento debido a su actividad física y desarrollo consume mayor cantidad de este elemento que las personas adultas, y es precisamente en esta edad en la que se debe procurar que sus niveles sean adecuados, ya que su desarrollo integral depende de ello.

La salud de la piel esta también vinculada a los correctos niveles de Zinc en el organismo, ya que, en conjunto con los procesos antes mencionados, la piel se vuelve resistente al ataque de agentes patógenos como acné, hongos, caspa, manchas, resequedad, dermatitis seborreica, herpes, melasma, soriasis y calvicie y muchas más.

El Zinc, al ser antimicótico, antimicrobiano, antiinflamatorio y antioxidante resulta ser un agente muy efectivo para eliminar la caída del cabello, generada por una o varias razones y revierte la pérdida, permitiendo la regeneración de las raíces capilares, permitiendo el crecimiento de nuevo cabello. Otras razones por las que se puede presentar calvicie es como resultado de alguna intervención quirúrgica, medicación o procesos infecciosos, en los que también ha resultado efectivo para recuperar la densidad de cabello.

El Zinc también ha sido identificado como importante elemento en la prevención de la Diabetes, ya que ayuda de manera muy efectiva a regular el nivel de azúcar en la sangre y mejora notablemente la sensibilidad a la insulina, protegiendo el páncreas de manera natural, manteniendo el órgano sano y con una correcta producción y secreción de la insulina.

Hablando de los efectos en el cuerpo para gente con Diabetes, reduce de manera notoria la gravedad de las Neuropatía Diabética, también reduce el nivel de colesterol y triglicéridos en sangre.

El Zinc, también está relacionado con la salud sexual, en el hombre el conteo seminal, motilidad y viabilidad de los espermatozoides que incide directamente en la fertilidad.

En la mujer se ha relacionado la deficiencia de Zinc con desequilibrios hormonales, problemas de función ovárica, menstruación irregular y definitivamente con la infertilidad.

Otro proceso en el que el Zinc tiene un papel de suma importancia es que funciona como defensa para el cerebro, ya que es responsable de no permitir la entrada al encéfalo a elementos que le resultan dañinos, como por ejemplo el Aluminio.

Una deficiencia de Zinc, permite el paso de elementos dañinos al interior del cerebro, que tal vez en otras partes del cuerpo no lo son, pero en los procesos cognitivos crean interferencias o lesiones que pueden ser detonantes para enfermedades como Parkinson o Alzheimer.

## Obtención del Zinc para la nutrición.

El zinc, al igual que la plata, es obtenido diariamente por medios naturales durante la alimentación a base de frutas y verduras, sin embargo, los cultivos de las verduras han desgastado la tierra y el tan preciado mineral ya no se encuentra en las cantidades que debería. El abono para la tierra más común es el NKP (Nitratos, Potasio y Fósforo), pero ¿alguien escuchó las palabras Zinc o Plata? Claro que no, volvemos a lo mismo, los abonos están diseñados para que las verduras crezcan más grandes y verdes, que se vean sanas y apetitosas y las compremos en la tienda, pero jamás fue diseñado el abono para que las verduras sean mas nutritivas.

El zinc lo podemos encontrar en forma de pastillas, inyecciones, gotas, cremas para aplicación tópica y adicionado en muchos alimentos, la mala noticia es que la absorción del Zinc no es tan sencilla como otros elementos y muchas veces el cuerpo lo elimina en su totalidad antes de aprovecharlo.

Estadísticamente la mejor manera de consumirlo ha sido, además de su forma natural en frutas y verduras, disuelto en agua alcalina en ayunas, ya que ese es el momento en que la absorción tiene la tasa más alta de todo el día.

Regresamos entonces al mismo punto que habíamos tocado con anterioridad, de los 8 vasos de agua recomendados para consumo diario, el primero es el más importante, y que además cumpla con las siguientes características:

Sea de agua alcalina

Contenga plata coloidal

Contenga Zinc

El resto del agua para consumo diario es importante, equilibrada y llena de minerales, pero ningún vaso tendrá la importancia del primero del día, lo que nos lleva a la importante pregunta:

**¿Qué calidad de agua le proporcionas a tu cuerpo a primera hora de la mañana?**

## DEFICIENCIAS DE ZINC

Son los niños y jóvenes en quienes se nota con mayor facilidad la deficiencia de Zinc sin necesidad de análisis clínicos, ya que presentan síntomas muy notorios como son:

- Gripas frecuentes
- Constantes infecciones de garganta
- Infecciones de estómago recurrentes
- Manchas blancas en las uñas de pies y manos
- Presencia de canas prematuras
- Infecciones en la piel
- Fatiga sin explicación aparente

**AGUA ALCALINA PARA BEBER.**

Alrededor del mundo, existen 8 manantiales naturales con suprema calidad de agua, estos manantiales se conocen desde tiempos remotos y son a los que la literatura bautizó como **"fuentes de la eterna juventud"**, y aunque un poco exagerado el término, no esta muy lejos de la realidad. Este nombramiento lo ganaron en base a que los pueblos que se alimentaban de estas fuentes naturales siempre fueron gente más sana y con apariencia más joven que los pueblos que no tenían acceso a ellos.

Aquí los nombres de los 8 manantiales de mayor pureza en el mundo.

1.  Viti Levú          Islas Fiyi
2.  Ölfos             Islandia
3.  San Pellegrino    Italia
4.  Reserva de        Sn Villavicencio Arg.
5.  Whakatane         Nueva Zelanda
6.  Chateldon         Francia
7.  Finé              Japón
8.  Konisaajo         Laponia Finlandesa

Algunos de estos manantiales embotellan su agua y la comercializan por el mundo, con precios por litro que van desde $ 5.00 usd hasta $ 300.00 usd, en botellas básicamente de cristal para que las características del preciado líquido no se pierdan en gran cantidad.

El agua embotellada siempre pierde calidad por las condiciones a las que se enfrenta en todas las horas de traslado, exposición al sol, cambios de temperatura, inmovilidad del líquido por confinamiento a un recipiente etc.

Existen otras plantas embotelladoras que aseguran tener calidad excepcional en el agua que venden, algunas de ellas hacen recolección de lluvia en zonas absolutamente alejadas de contaminación y que obtienen agua con características únicas, otras cuantas, recaban agua de manantiales y les dan un proceso adicional para convertir el agua pura en un agua súper pura.

A final de cuentas, es importante buscar el agua de excelente calidad para llevarla a nuestro seno familiar, en busca de salud ya bienestar de los miembros de nuestra familia.

Nuevamente buscando una solución, encontré en el mercado un sistema de purificación que nos brinda los beneficios de la alcalinidad, la plata coloidal y Zinc entre otros elementos, además de agua de extraordinaria calidad por la ausencia de hongos, virus, bacterias y otros microorganismos patógenos en un solo momento, y claro, perfectamente comparable con la calidad de los mejores y mas puros manantiales del planeta.

Por todas éstas bondades simultáneas considero que sí existe un sistema de purificación de agua que merece ser reconocido como el máximo representante de los sistemas de purificación integrales que ofrecen ciencia al servicio de la salud y bienestar.

La ventaja de tener en casa un sistema de purificación de alta calidad es que nuestra familia tendrá acceso de manera prácticamente ilimitada a agua con la calidad de los manantiales mas puros del planeta sin tener que pagar grandes sumas de dinero por cada litro que se consuma, con el plus, que el agua no pierde sus características debido al acarreo.

Analicemos a detalle un muy bien conocido a nivel mundial, sistema de purificación de agua de una compañía japonesa que cuenta con una gran cantidad de tecnologías para lograr el precioso líquido con calidad insuperable incluso por los manantiales antes mencionados.

Examinemos algunas de las tecnologías que posee en su diseño y cómo colaboran en conjunto para lograr un agua de calidad suprema.

El sistema de purificación de agua del que hago mención, funciona por medio de flujo de filtración por gravedad, de la misma manera que la filtración natural presente en todos los manantiales del mundo.

I.-   El primer paso es a través de una esponja con una capacidad de filtración de partículas de hasta 1 micrómetro, es decir la milésima parte de un milímetro, que elimina gran cantidad de impurezas, así como microorganismos de tamaño mayor.


II.-  La segunda etapa corresponde al paso a través del cartucho de carbón activado por medio de gravedad, este contiene varias tecnologías que se detallan a continuación:

**Carbón activado:** Elimina olores y colores, cloro, compuestos orgánicos, detergentes y productos químicos.

**Carbón activado impregnado con Magnesio:** Ioniza el agua y mejora su potencial antioxidante.

**Carbón activado impregnado con Plata:** Elimina bacterias, rompe su ciclo de reproducción e inhibe el desarrollo de huevecillos.

**Material KDF:** Los Medios de proceso **KDF**-55 son gránulos de cobre-

Zinc de alta pureza que usan redox (el intercambio de electrones) para eliminar el fierro y el sulfuro de hidrógeno, los metales pesados solubles en agua y microorganismos.

**RESINA DE INTERCAMBIO IÓNICO**: Remueve metales pesados, adiciona iones de Sodio y Potasio para mejorar la calidad del agua.

**GRÁNULOS DE ARCILLA, ESFERAS DE BIOPLATA Y MINERALES**: Filtran contaminantes y liberan minerales que ayudan a incrementar y estabilizar el PH del agua.

**ARENA DE SÍLICE**: Estabiliza y mantiene en equilibrio el PH al agua.

III.- En la tercera etapa, el fluido líquido se almacena en un depósito que contiene:

**PIEDRAS MINERALES Y PIEDRAS IMPREGNADAS CON PLATA Y ZINC**: Las funciones de este conjunto de piedras es:

- ✓ Prevenir el crecimiento de hongos, bacterias o virus en el agua almacenada.
- ✓ Liberar oxígeno
- ✓ Mineralizar el agua con elementos benéficos para el hombre.

IV.- Por último, tecnología de magnetismo para organizar las moléculas de agua en forma hexagonal, de la misma manera que tenemos organizadas las moléculas dentro de nuestro cuerpo

Con esa estructura, el agua se vuelve de fácil absorción pues se integra de manera perfecta a otros fluidos corporales y penetra las paredes celulares de manera sencilla.

La estructura hexagonal del agua en la naturaleza la podemos apreciar fácilmente en la geometría de los copos de nieve.

## ¿Agua alcalina para bañarme?

Pues sí, existe esa posibilidad, pero:

## ¿POR QUÉ SERÍA NECESARIO?

Vamos a contestar esta pregunta primero con una observación.

¿Se ha dado cuenta que al salir de la regadera la piel se siente tan reseca que necesitamos untarnos alguna crema humectante para quitarnos esa sensación?

Es absurdo, pero una realidad, salir de la regadera y que nuestra piel tenga una sensación de resequedad o deshidratación. Desgraciadamente estamos tan acostumbrados a ello que no nos preguntamos si eso es normal, y en realidad no lo es.

Al meternos a la ducha, el agua que recibimos del sistema de agua municipal o Hidrosistemas, esta tan lleno de químicos, contaminantes y toxinas que nuestro cuerpo al percibir la presencia de estos, reacciona ante ella como una amenaza, cerrando los poros y estresando la superficie del tejido.

El poro cerrado no permite la eliminación de toxinas y tampoco la hidratación, no hay intercambio de fluidos por lo que el baño es sólo superficial, no importa que tanto restreguemos el jabón, el poro sigue cerrado.

Al terminar el baño, la piel sigue tensa, estresada pues está haciendo un esfuerzo por mantener el poro cerrado hasta que le untamos algún elemento o crema humectante y relajante, pero la hidratación correcta no se llevó a cabo, pues las cremas no sustituyen al agua natural, y tampoco se llevó a cabo la eliminación de toxinas, que, a lo largo del tiempo, envenenan y envejecen a nuestra piel, haciéndola propicia a que se instalen en ella enfermedades derivadas de bacterias, hongos o virus.

## ¿Cómo sería éste mismo escenario si cambiamos el tipo de agua?

La piel al recibir agua alcalina, libre de químicos y otros contaminantes, abre y relaja al poro, pues reconoce al líquido como algo benéfico y se prepara para hacer el intercambio de fluidos mediante el cual elimina las toxinas por medio de la secreción por los poros y bebe agua para la correcta hidratación de todas las capas de la piel.

## El resultado:

Piel más sana, hidratada, regenerada, joven y relajada.

La piel que usualmente está en contacto con ducha de agua pura y alcalina tiene una regeneración celular más activa, las células están efectivamente más sanas y mejor nutridas, y como resultado visible, las personas que cuentan con una ducha como ésta, se ven de 10 a 15 años más jóvenes, tienen menos o cero enfermedades de la piel.

# CONCLUSIÓN

## *MUNDO ACUÁTICO*

Después de abordar esta gran cantidad de temas relacionados el agua y la vida en la tierra, la vida saludable del ser humano y todos los matices que podría tener el agua y la manera en que pueden impactar en la vida de las personas, las conclusiones también pueden ser muchas y muy variadas.

A manera de resumen, me gustaría reclcar la importancia de un agua con características especiales para el óptimo desarrollo del hombre y el buen funcionamiento de todos sus sistemas.

El tipo de agua que consumimos y los minerales que debería tener para que esa agua no solo cumpla con el papel de hidratación del cuerpo, sino que sea un verdadero alimento a nivel celular, deben ser definitivamente de una calidad excepcional, libre de toxinas y rica en minerales.

La ausencia de todos éstos nutrientes del agua, repercutirán definitivamente en provocar un cuerpo débil, con baja  o nula capacidad de defenderse de agentes patógenos, dejaremos nuestro propio cuerpo a la deriva, generando un envejecimiento celular prematuro y que en algún momento convergerá en un colapso general de sistemas respiratorio, circulatorio, digestivo, respiratorio y /o central.

El agua, es un tema que ha fascinado a cientos de científicos en los últimos 100 años, y a múltiples investigadores de todas partes del mundo.

Existen hoy día, hospitales que tienen tratamientos especializados para ciertos pacientes exclusivamente con agua con la calidad de la que hemos estado hablando, las unidades de quemados que les están rociando agua con ésta pureza cada ciertos minutos durante semanas, y sin necesidad de añadir medicamentos alópatas, homeópatas, o de alguna otra índole, logran la regeneración de tejidos hasta en la tercera parte del tiempo que lo harían bajo otras circunstancias sin lidiar con la presencia de infecciones por hongos o bacterias.

Otro ejemplo de centros de recuperación que utilizan esta calidad de agua, son centros médicos especializados en los riñones, que se ven dañados por diversas razones, incluso por origen bacteriano o viral, son tratados con flujo de agua alcalina rica en minerales especiales, que limpian los riñones y permiten la reparación de los tejidos, eliminación de agentes patógenos causantes de las lesiones, favorecen la nutrición de las células  al grado que han experimentado una regeneración celular importante y como resultado, el órgano recupera su operabilidad hasta un 100%.

# BIBLIOGRAFÍA

**Bohinski, Robert C.** *"Bioquímica"* México: Editorial Addison-Wesley Iberoamericana

**Carlos M. Requejo.** *"La casa enferma: energías telúricas y salud."* Editorial: Didaco S.A.

**Carlos M. Requejo.** *"Estrés de alta tensión: Contaminación electromagnética."* Editorial: Didaco S.A.

**K.Piatkin, Yu. Krivoshein.** *"Microbiología"*. Moscú: Editorial Mir.

**Fieser y Fieser.** *"Química orgánica"*. México: Editorial Grijalbo.

**Pérez Salazar Salvador M**. *"Introducción a la Química y el ambiente"* México: Publicaciones Cultural.

*"El cuerpo Humano"*. Colección Científica de Time Life.

*"La mente"*. Colección Científica de Time Life.

# INVESTIGACIÓN EN INTERNET.

## Salud y terapias naturales:

http://www.enbuenasmanos.com/articulos/muestra.asp?art=6


## Ciencia y salud.

http://www.dsalud.com/numero102_2.htm

http://www.aguayaire.com/t-26.htm

## Psicología.

http://psicologia.laguia2000.com/general/la-enfermedad-mental

http://www.juntadeandalucia.es/averroes/~29701428/salud/mental2.htm

http://www.meddir.net/enfermedades%
20mentales.htm

http://es.wikipedia.org/wiki/Enfermeda
d_mental

**Cáncer, toxinas y dioxinas.**

http://www.euskalnet.net/alobizirik/dio
xinas.htm

http://www.monografias.com/trabajos6
1/dioxinas/dioxinas.shtml

www.ingramcontent.com/pod-product-compliance
Lightning Source LLC
Chambersburg PA
CBHW070810240726
48654CB00007B/281